e-Purchasing *plus*

Changing the Way Corporations Buy

To contact the Authors
Or for ordering information
Visit our Web site
http://www.epurchasingplus.com

e-Purchasing *plus*

Changing the Way Corporations Buy

Larry C. Giunipero
Chris Sawchuk

From the Book Reader
(America's most independent review of new books)

If you are the purchasing manager of a new company, issue the first PO for this new book...

This is a thorough book, 200+ pages, filled with - here's how - experience from IBM, Cisco, Dell, Amazon, Staples. G.E. and others who are blazing trails...Zinger chapters that show impact, define the relationships, reveal how to catch up or get ahead using B to B and e-commerce.

From an eProcurement / SAP Consultant

It pulls together information from hundreds of sources to present a clear understanding of the impact technology is having on the purchasing function. I am particular pleased with the authors approach in using test cases throughout the book...The book is for all purchasing professionals regardless of their level of knowledge of the Internet and ERP systems.

Library of Congress Cataloging-in-Publication Data

Giunipero, Larry C.
        e-Purchasing Plus /Larry C. Giunipero
Sawchuk, Chris
        e-Purchasing Plus / Chris Sawchuk

The contents of this book reflect the authors' opinions only and unless otherwise
stated in the book, does not in any way reflect nor represent the companies
named in the book.

With a great deal of gratitude, we dedicate this book to
Gerrie C. Kalka and Jan Giunipero
*whose support and encouragement made this text
happen and in memory of **Frank Giunipero** whose
courage was a source of inspiration.*

The visual appearance and layout would not be possible
without the extensive contribution of Kim Haidacher
(Author's daughter) who provided the
cover design, textbook layout and expertise in taking
the book from our notes to a complete text.

We would also like to thank Robbie Bendorf of
Bendorf & Associates for his many contributions.

And finally, we want to thank Gerald Antonette who
had the vision to do this project.

Order Form

Visit our web site for online ordering (to include credit cards) and to receive a **free excerpt** of **e-Purchasing** *plus*.

www.epurchasingplus.com

Or, fill out the form below and mail to **JGC Enterprises, 4 Candlewood Drive, Goshen, NY 10924.**

Please send ___ copies of **e-Purchasing** *plus* at $39.95 each. Please add postage and handling ($4.95 for 1st book and $1.50 for each additional) and local sales tax for NY orders only. If I am not completely satisfied, I will return the book(s) for a full refund within 15 days. Satisfaction unconditionally guaranteed.

Name_____

Company/Institution _____

Address_____

City_____State_____ Zip _____

Daytime Phone # _____

Email_____

For quantity discount call 845-291-8141

Payment Options (please check one):

(   ) Check or Money Order Enclosed
I am enclosing my check or money order, payable to JGC Enterprises. I understand I will receive my book(s) within two (2) weeks. I have included $4.50 postage and handling for the first book ordered, $1.50 for each additional book, plus local sales tax for NY only. (Please check one):

_____VISA   _____MASTERCARD   _____AMEX

Account # _____

Expiration Date_____

Signature _____

(   ) Purchase Order and Bill Me
Fill the enclosed purchase order and bill me the cost of the book(s), plus postage, handling and local sales tax. Please include phone number for confirmation.

Contents
(Summary)

Contents

Section 2: Making e-Purchasing *plus* a Reality:

Section 3: ERP Systems & e-Purchasing *plus* Solution Providers:

Agentics	Supply Channel
American Software	ECON/Purchasing
Ariba	Operating Resource Management System (ORMS)
Aspect	eXplore 2000 -- eDesign, eSource, and eOperate
Baan	E-Enterprise suite
Brio	Brio ONE
BuyerZone	e-Catalog Central and Get a Quote.
Chemdex Corp	
Clarus	E-Procurement
Commerce One	BuySite 5.0
ConnectInc.com	MarketStream
Dazel	Web Delivery for Purchasing

Section 4: The Future of e-Purchasing

An Open Letter To Purchasing Professionals

Technology is having a major impact on our profession by:

- changing the way corporations buy.
- elevating Purchasing to a strategic level.
- fulfilling Purchasing visions.

e-Purchasing *plus* is the set of tools available for purchasing professionals to use in order to take advantage of the new technologies. These dramatic changes to the way corporations buy are creating new purchasing opportunities: Purchasers now have immediate worldwide access to suppliers creating new and unlimited sources and the information age permits continual/real time communications with suppliers never before available.

Although the major driver of technological change is the Internet, the transition to e-Purchasing *plus* cannot just include "using the Internet," but must incorporate a total change in process for the corporation. The transformation requires the use of at least the following tools:

1. Enterprise Resource Planning (ERP) - the combining of the technologies from computers with the massively complex programs from ERP software companies, such as SAP, Baan, and Oracle
2. The Internet itself

Elevating Purchasing to a Strategic Level

Is e-Purchasing *plus* the new weapon that will elevate Purchasing to a strategic function in our corporations? We believe the answer is YES. Technology is not only providing the capability to enhance Purchasing's value to an organization; it's also providing the visibility for management to view Purchasing as a key component in the running of our businesses. Purchasing is no longer viewed as a back office operation, but now becomes a strategic force in the business.

Fulfilling Purchasing Visions

Imagine that you are the chief procurement officer of a multinational corporation. Also imagine that at the touch of a button you are able to see the performance of all your worldwide purchasing organizations every day, including orders placed, savings achieved, supplier-delivery performance, cash payments to suppliers, quality of product delivered by suppliers, and other key areas appropriate to measuring the performance of your purchasing organizations. e-Purchasing *plus* provides the technology to achieve this vision.

The technology for the information age is changing so rapidly that before we finished writing this book, some of the information will be obsolete. However, it is important to assess the current situation and understand the changes occurring in our field. Thus we can implement appropriate actions necessary to *begin* to take advantage of this dynamic change.

The purpose of this book is to provide the purchasing professional with the information needed to understand how technology is transforming the purchasing function.

The reader will also:
- understand how the information age is changing purchasing.
- learn from the actual experiences of many companies, including IBM, Motorola, AT&T, Lucent, and small- to medium-sized businesses.
- understand e-Purchasing *plus*'s impact on acquisition strategies, measurements, supplier relationships, and the role of purchasing.
- understand the relationship between the supply chain and e-Purchasing *plus*.
- tap into a wealth of e-Purchasing *plus* tools.
- understand SAP, the software system that both large and medium-sized companies are turning to.

Good luck on your endeavors.

Gerald, Larry & Chris

Section 1
The e-Purchasing *plus* Environment

1
The Brave New World of e-Purchasing

Changing Purchasing Forever

The field of purchasing has been *changed forever* by the development and commercialization of Internet-based technologies. The question is, are you ready for these changes? The purpose of this book is to help you get ready regardless of whether you are a novice with the technology, one who has dabbled in it, or an expert. This book is intended to help the novice understand and use these powerful technological tools as well as to improve the skills of more experienced users. Internet-related technologies may have more to do with moving purchasing out of the back room and into the boardroom than any other development the field has experienced in the 20th century.

Experts in strategic management have argued that an organization's non-core operations should be outsourced. [1] Properly applying these Internet technologies will enable the purchasing function to move toward a more strategic posture by finally freeing

3

it from its clerical role and allowing employees more time to focus on more value-adding activities; perhaps purchasing can even be saved from being outsourced.

e-Purchasing is the buying piece of the equation that will enable purchasing to move into a more value-added orientation. The traditional industry view of the purchasing function centers around administrative, transaction-based processes. This viewpoint drives organizations to focus on the efficiency of the purchasing process (expense) and misses the real opportunities in effectiveness (cost/price).

A select group of firms is focusing on e-Purchasing as part of their overall e-business strategy. One is IBM, whose vice president and chief purchasing officer, Gene Ritcher, stated. "Our goal is to drive the rapid transition of purchasing into an IBM showcase for e-business. The Internet offers vast opportunities for cost savings, collaboration, market-intelligence gathering, and improved transaction processing."

Excerpts from a recent New York Times article by Steve Lohr further illustrate the impact of e-Purchasing. "As a wired Silicon Valley company, of course, Cisco can move its business-to-business dealings onto the Internet sooner than many others." But Peter Solvik, Cisco's chief information officer, insists that before long companies in any field can do the same. "As the Internet gets fully deployed," he said, "what we're doing is going to become commonplace. Business-to-business commerce is the killer application on the Internet."

In order to gain the biggest opportunity for using Internet technology soon, companies will have to shift focus from the visions to the details inside the gray offices of corporate America, where workers handle chores like purchasing, customer service, and employee benefits. These tasks make up many of the nuts-and-bolts operations of the modern economy, consuming millions of hours of labor and hundreds of billions of dollars. If such work can be made more efficient, the economic payoff could be considerable. No wonder companies have come to view Internet technology as a communications tool that can reduce the expense of many transactions, whether buying factory equipment from outside suppliers or processing expense accounts. [2]

Nicholas Donofrio, senior vice president of technology and manufacturing at IBM, says, "Our global purchasing operation is making a tremendous difference to the company. [It is] saving the company millions. They [the purchasing group] are an incredibly competent, dedicated group of professionals." Purchasing, however, has not always been held in such high esteem by management. "Purchasers now add value. They question and challenge engineering and manufacturing judgments of people. They suggest ways to do things differently, and they build supplier partnerships around the world."

Donofrio says that purchasing has become more strategic to IBM and will become even more strategic in the future once IBM's purchasing process moves to the Internet. "The vast majority of our expenditures are going to be done via the Internet," says Donofrio. "There will be an exception process when something can't be purchased over the Internet. We process 5 million pieces of paper per year. Within the next few years that will go to zero. We intend to wipe out paper as part of our transaction process," he says. IBM's Internet purchasing initiative will reduce cost and purchasing cycle time and will free up buyers to work on more important issues.[3]

Business Model Changes

These previous examples illustrate that e-Purchasing will bring changes. Change is here, it is coming, and there is no reason to fight it. The Internet is a major force that will change our individual and business lives for the foreseeable future. One author predicts that by the year 2015, 50 percent of Gross National Product will be related to electronic Commerce. [4] Another writer compares the Internet to the advent of the radio in the early 20th century. "Radio created more than a product or an industry," he wrote. "It had a huge impact on the society of the 1920's. It changed the way the average person thought about distance and time. Simultaneity no longer required proximity. Global events could be experienced as they happened, performances in distant cities could be heard, and news and weather were available at the switch of a dial." The radio changed the way we lived and work and so will the Internet. [5]

New Business Model at Dell

Dell Computer and its founder Michael Dell have created a business system that is the envy of many organizations that utilize the old business models. Dell has a rapid build-to-order system that enables the firm to ship all its product directly to the end customer without the need for expensive distribution or retail systems. Dell's use of the Internet to communicate with suppliers and customers allows it to speed its products to its customers and receive payment before paying its suppliers. Its business model, by one account, generates a 160% return on invested capital. [6] In Dell's model, electronic communication permits efficient linkages in the supply chain, from customer to manufacturer to the suppliers. In Michael Dell's words, "So if you've got an operation that builds a component, the cost to communicate with that operation in an information sense goes to zero. That means you can build a linkage between a components supplier and a manufacturer and make it very, very efficient. That requires that you scale more quickly and gives you more flexibility; you can manage a supplier network in a more dynamic fashion and get things off your balance sheet that are your Specialty." [7] Dell's system is geared to assessing continuously their suppliers' performance and manufacturing things quickly in response to customer demand. The manufacturing cycle time to build a Dell Computer is three to four hours. The process is designed to minimize the number of human touches and maximize the use of time. Extra time and extra steps in processes all add to inventory.

Suppliers are treated as extensions of Dell, so the purchasing personnel at Dell are extensively involved in understanding their suppliers' operations, products, and commodities. Adds Dell, If we tell our suppliers, "Hey look. You need to deliver at 6:20 a.m. and you have to come to this dock, and it's got to be this high," they say, "Yes sir." [8] Dell has a focused supplier base with 25 suppliers providing 85% of their annual purchase dollar expenditure.

These manufacturing and purchasing practices keep inventory in the supply chain to a minimum and enable the firm to generate large cash returns. Dell's five lessons from the new model are: 1) Use the Internet to lower the cost of developing links among manufacturers and suppliers and customers; 2) Turn over to outsiders operations that aren't central to the business; 3) Accelerate the pace of change, and condition employees to accept change;
4) Experiment with Internet businesses and develop trials to see what happens when customers can access information in ways they never could before; and 5) Consider what to do with investment that

Comparing the Traditional and New Business Models	
Traditional Business Model	**New Business Model**
Based on traditional technologies and personal contacts	Based on electronically based communication and relationships
High investment in assets	Lower investment in assets
Standardized products in large volumes	Made to order based on customer demand
High transaction costs in information acquisition, cross-organizational communication, purchase orders, crossing national boundaries	Low transaction costs in information acquisition, cross-organizational communication, purchase orders, crossing national boundaries
High inventories in the supply chain	Rapid information flow replaces inventory
Supply base managed but large	Focused and flexible supply base
Numerous levels of management	Few levels of management
Inter-organizational information flow restricted	Free flow of inter-organizational information
Focus on profits	Focus on growth, cash returns, and profits

Exhibit 1-1 - Traditional and New Business Models

could be freed up by using inventory and other assets now on the balance sheet.[9]

Using the models created by Dell, Amazon.com, Cisco Systems, and others, we have developed a chart that compares the old and new business models. It should provide the reader with a general idea of where these new business models have advantages over the more traditional business models. (Exhibit 1-1)

The new model provides many advantages to those who adopt it. First and foremost in a free market system are the returns on cash and assets. Second, the ability to generate sales without having an extensive distribution network is impressive. On-line models are geared toward using the Internet technologies to advance a business, which pleases its customers without having to carry inventory to do it. This enables the firm to price its products competitively and still give its customers their desired products within a reasonable cycle time.

Applying the Business-Direct Model to Car Sales

The pace at which change is occurring toward the new business model is exemplified by the actions of two old line automobile manufacturers, General Motors Corporation and Ford Motor Corporation. The automobile sector represents the traditional model of American business. It has high capital investments in plant and equipment. Its dealer network carries on average 60 to 90 days' worth of inventory and its workers are highly paid and unionized. They have massive supply-chain inventories, not only at the dealers, but in transit, in process at the plants, and from their suppliers.

Both these firms see the Internet --specifically electronic commerce--as a way to slash their cost structure and serve their customers better. The long-term dream at GM is to turn the company into an organization that could receive a customer's on-line order and deliver him a new car or truck in several days.[10] Thus both firms are moving quickly to move to an electronic-based system, both for customer interface and in doing business with their suppliers. General Motors has linked up with Commerce One, Inc., and will call its Web site "TradeXchange," while Ford has contracted with Oracle for its site called "autoXchange." "By the end of 2001 we're going to expect all of General Motors' purchases to go through this site and we would expect all our suppliers to be actively engaged," said Harold Kurtner, GM's purchasing chief. This amounts to a lot of business, considering the firm spends 87 billion a year with 30,000 suppliers. Ford expenditures are also in this range, making these two corporations the biggest purchasers in the United States behind the federal government.

General Motors wants its suppliers to use the site to buy common items that it purchases so these suppliers can get the advantages of GM's pricing. For example, a company that provides suspension parts to GM could use the virtual marketplace to get a more favorable price on steel.[11] Both firms feel that the electronic business format will save them millions of dollars now spent on placing hundreds of thousands of individual purchase orders at an estimated cost of $100 per order. There are also other costs--making personal contacts, invoicing, etc.--that could be saved under the new format.

The ultimate goal of these two traditional companies is to implement an on-line business model similar to Michael Dell's. In this new model, cars would be built to order, eliminating billions of dollars in carrying costs. Warranty problems would be reported on line from service shops and corrected on the assembly line. Meanwhile, suppliers would ship parts as needed and receive on-line schedules to enable the smooth flow of material to the assembly plants.

This changing environment and how purchasers adapt to it is the focus of this book. Purchasing in corporate America is changing and will be changed as the use of Internet technologies in conducting business-to-business transactions becomes more common.

Adapting Internet Technologies in Purchasing

It is our view that organizations will adopt this technology at varying rates. Some organizations may initially resist and dismiss the Internet as a fad or trend that will eventually fade away. Other organizations will explore how they can use this technology in limited ways, and still others will aggressively pursue the technology and see it as a strategy to gain competitive advantage over other firms. Because of this non-uniformity in adoption, this text will help you understand the technology and how it can be used to run your purchasing organization more efficiently and effectively. Remember that even if you aren't considering e-Purchasing, your competitors are moving to adopt e-Commerce models. According to Forrester Research, in 1998 business-to-business electronic commerce accounted for 78 percent of all Internet purchases, totaling an estimated $17 billion. Forrester predicts that total business-to-business Internet transactions will exceed $327 billion by the year 2002.

While there are technical differences that we will explain later, the terms "World Wide Web" and "Internet" are used interchangeably in this text. As with any new technology, the extent of adaptation and use will depend on the resources available, skill level of the personnel using it, and the extent of support by top management. Marketing theory suggests that when a new product or service is introduced there are several stages in the adoption process. Exhibit 1-2 illustrates the five stages of the adoption process.

Exhibit 1-2

Stages in the e-Purchasing Adoption Process
Innovators Ŀ Early Adapters Ŀ Early Majority Ŀ Late Majority Ŀ Laggards

Innovators are the first to adopt a new technology, and these individuals are not afraid to take risks. They search for information and rely on other innovators or hard evidence that they have often sought out prior to adopting a technology. Amazon.com is a good example of an innovator with regard to Internet technology. In fact when someone mentions the Internet, many automatically think of Amazon.com first. This firm changed the traditional business model of bricks, mortar, and warehouses to a vertical corporation model that utilizes the Internet as a marketing and ordering vehicle with very little physical investment. The firm relies on traditional businesses in the order fulfillment process of physically getting the purchased items to its customers.

Early adapters are the next to embrace the technology, and often they are specialty firms. A good example of this is Dell Computer, which used its knowledge of computers and the Internet to set up a buy-direct organization and now runs its supply chain over the Internet. The Dell model is now considered the standard for the personal-computer business, and attempts to emulate it are being made by competitors such as Compaq and Hewlett-Packard. The problem is that when these firms establish direct-buy models of business, they cannibalize the sales of their distributors and retailers, but the overriding need to compete and grow effectively requires this action.

Early-majority adapters want to avoid risk and consider the product or service only after many early adapters have tried it. An example of an early majority is a firm like Grainger, Inc., a traditional industrial distributor that now does extensive business-to-business transactions over its web site. Many readers of the text will be in the early-majority category.

Late-majority adapters are cautious about new ideas and more conservative about using a new technology until it has been extensively proven. Compaq could be considered a late-majority example, as they adopted the direct-sell model only after Dell, Micron, and Gateway had already set up their business models in this fashion. Late majority adapters such as Compaq may be loyal to their existing distribution structure, which may partially explain some of the late-majority behavior.

Laggards prefer to do things the way they have been done in the past and are very suspicious of new ideas. Readers of this text who are in laggard-type organizations can hopefully justify to their management the advantages of this new technology. If the adaptation or implementation of a new product or technology results in much higher costs, lower benefits, and more problems than originally anticipated, laggards may actually look shrewd in their conservatism. [12]

In addition to the previously mentioned example of Dell Computer, other firms like IBM, Cisco Systems, and General Electric are also considered early adapters of Internet technologies and are aggressively using the Internet within and outside the walls of their organizations. General Electric's "Trading Partner Network" (TPN) is considered one of the leaders in e-purchasing. IBM and Dell use Internet-based purchasing to run their supply-chain-management programs.

Assessing Your Internet Strategy

A purchaser's use and application of the Internet is almost endless. Determining where you are now and where you would like to be in the future can be assessed by looking at the matrix in Exhibit 1-3.

e-Purchasing Stages

	Transactional Approach Savings are realized by placing small dollar orders on the Internet *(Phase II)*	Integrated Automated Enterprise e-Purchasing is part of a total net-worked business model in the supply chain *(Phase IV)*
High		
Low	Search-and-Find Approach Uses the Internet as a tool to locate suppliers and check financials, inventory, lines carried, etc *(Phase I)*	Cost-Driver Approach The Internet is used in conjunction with intranets and extranets to lower purchase costs and to distribute information *(Phase III)*
	Low	High

Number of Purchasing Tasks

Use of Internet Technology

Exhibit 1-3

Remember that Exhibit 1 is only a guide, but it will help you understand why e-Purchasing is important, for these Internet technologies will not be adopted uniformly. To illustrate this point with another technology, only about 50% of the world's population has ever made a telephone call.

Regarding the Exhibit, in Phase 1 the purchaser is using the Internet as a device to help search the marketplace. Activities in this phase include visiting supplier Web sites, browsing the Thomas Register for sources, and checking Dun & Bradstreet's (D&B) on-line reports for financial information. On-line catalogues with product offerings are scanned, and even the annual report can be read. The Thomas Register is one of the buyer's main sources of information about new suppliers, and it is available either on line or on CD-ROM. Checking the Security and Exchange's EDGAR database or D&B's on-line service to verify a supplier's financial data is also useful. In Phase 1 the purchaser is using the Internet for early-stage sourcing activities. This is very similar to individuals who spend their nights logging onto Web sites that are of interest.

As the comfort level and familiarity grow with the use of the Internet, the purchaser moves to Phase II and places purchase orders for low-dollar items, which traditionally require high transaction costs. Examples of these items include MRO, office, and laboratory supplies. In all likelihood there is currently a small-dollar order system in place, which includes purchasing cards, blanket orders, or systems contracts. The Internet technologies provide a new, more efficient option for handling such items.

Often a natural transition is made from one of these small-dollar systems to the supplier's own Web site. There are many well-developed Web sites in these product areas. For example, Grainger (www.grainger.com) for MRO items, and Staples (www.staples.com) for office supplies. The purchaser places an order on one of these sites and quickly begins to realize the advantages offered. The ease of the transaction in terms of locating items, quick response to user needs, and the comfort of knowing the transaction was securely completed at a very low transaction cost all help lead to expansion of Internet buys. During the later stages of Phase II, several secure Internet trading sites that allow access to multiple suppliers may be approached. These include long-time Internet providers such as Fisher Technology Group and Ariba.

In Phase III the purchaser and management begin to view the Internet as not only a way to save transaction costs, but also to achieve greater price/cost savings. Now the purchaser may use the Internet to solicit bids or contract the services of a business-to-business on-line bid-auction provider such as Free Markets, Inc., of Pittsburgh (www.freemarkets.com). At this stage the firm is realizing not only transactional savings but also cost/price savings because of the intensely competitive bid process. Usually in this phase the firm is applying Internet bidding to basic and standardized commodities versus critical highly engineered components. Late in this phase the development of extranets and intranets are started and used to distribute information both externally and internally.

Phase IV is the most advanced and integrated e-Purchasing strategy and requires that the entire firm adopt a new business model. e-Purchasing is a part of a total-supply-chain effort extending from the final customer back to a firms suppliers. This new automated, extended-enterprise model is used to drive the firm to superior performance, which is supported by top management. A typical activity during this phase is installing or refining the ERP system. A plan is undertaken to modify and re-engineer existing business processes to fit the new technology. Intranets (internal networks) are refined to transmit internal corporate data such as purchase policies, available training, job postings, purchase-order forms, internal part numbers, and specifications. Extranets (eternal networks) are also refined to insure that there is a secure environment for exchanging information with key suppliers.

The organizational vision is focused on managing its suppliers, business operations, and customers through Internet-based technologies. The benefits of efficient operations, reduced cost, and faster cycle times throughout the supply chain are the ultimate goal. While many firms see this technology as the future and are committing resources necessary to make it to Phase IV, very few have achieved this status. Even leading companies such as IBM, Dell, Cisco, and General Electric, which would be categorized as Phase IV, are continually upgrading and improving their systems in an effort to stay at the leading edge of the e-purchasing and e-business movement.

General Electric reported that last year it purchased $1 billion worth of goods and services via the Internet, and it expects to reach $5 billion by next year. General Electric is constructing a massive extranet to handle billions of dollars in purchasing and, in the process, force tens of thousands of its suppliers to conduct business on the Internet. GE plans to launch trading extranets for each of its 12 operating units. The systems could serve as many as 40,000 trading partners by 2002, a GE executive confirmed, all of which would have to use the network in order to do business with the 91-billion-dollar company.

By converting some $5 billion in capital spending to an extranet within four years, GE stands to become one of the largest Internet-based buyers. The benefits could amount to more than bragging rights. If GE makes good on its plans--and some experts say that's a big "if"--the extranet strategy could dramatically boost GE's bottom line by reducing costs, according to Randy Rowe, manager of GE's corporate initiatives group. "Today, we have too many purchasing systems to count," Rowe said. "We're looking to enable each division to manage its purchasing on extranets, with financial data funneling to a centralized platform." At full deployment, GE could save between $500 million and $750 million through reduced errors, contract leverage that results in lower costs, and other efficiencies.[13]

e-Business, e-Commerce, and e-Purchasing Differences

By now it should be clear that there are many paths to electronic business and each organization will be at a different point in its development and use of these technologies. In this text

electronic business is defined as *those activities utilizing Internet and other technologies* that enable an organization to become networked. The implementation of e-business will require the use of several technologies such as the Internet, extranets, intranets, ERP systems, and database access among trading partners. E-business will provide the firm a solution to manage effectively both its internal and external linkages. These include activities involved with supply-chain management, customer service, customer management, planning, and inventory systems. Finally, e-business will require an organization to re-engineer its processes to accommodate these new technologies.

   Electronic commerce is defined as *conducting business transactions with suppliers and customers electronically*. The major electronic transfer mechanisms are the Internet, an extranet, or an EDI system. However, a broader view could include faxes, e-mail, or other electronic forms. The focus in this text is on Internet-based and extranet-type exchanges that we feel will be the leading technologies of electronic commerce in the future.

   Electronic purchasing/e-Purchasing *comprises the actions taken by the purchasing organization to integrate Internet-based technologies into its role of managing the upstream portion of the supply chain in order to reduce costs and time and increase productivity.*

Market Opportunities and Purchasing Advantages

   As previously mentioned, growth of business-to-business transactions on the Internet is expected to explode. Estimates indicate that 50% of US Gross Domestic Product (GDP) is suitable for Web-based buying. Forrester Research estimates that by 2003 one and one-third (1.33) trillion dollars' worth of business will be conducted on the Internet. This figure is still only 25% of total GDP. According to Forrester, in 1998 business-to-business electronic commerce accounted for 78 percent of total Internet purchases and totaled an estimated $17 billion. This data show that there is a lot of room for growth in the area of Web-based buying.

e-Purchasing can: (1) reduce transaction costs; (2) increase accuracy and speed; (3) provide better information for managers; (4) free time to develop strategies. However, important issues must be addressed before implementing an e-Purchasing solution. DeLano and Tibbens of Mercer Consulting Group illustrate the potential of e-Purchasing to improve the process through an example. Let's assume that a maintenance technician needs an additional part to complete a repair. Here are the steps to procure that part through an e-Purchasing system:

1. The technician accesses the corporate Internet and goes to an electronic, Web-based catalog that contains information on parts from multiple vendors.
2. The technician searches for the required item (perhaps using a keyword search) and checks specification, price, stock availability, and delivery lead-time. With a few clicks of the mouse, a purchase requisition is completed.
3. The purchase requisition is automatically captured in the company's ERP system, and, if required, routed directly to the appropriate person for approval.
4. A purchase order is sent electronically to the supplier's system. The supplier's system confirms price and availability and immediately sends a delivery confirmation back to the technician's mailbox.
5. The supplier ships the part according to the instructions on the purchase order and it arrives the same or next day.
6. The invoice, when received from the supplier, is automatically matched with the purchase order and paid without any further approvals.

This electronic system provides important benefits for both the buyer and the supplier. The buyer can reduce purchasing costs, increase speed of acquisition, and significantly reduce paperwork and administrative costs. In addition, the buying organization can better control "non-contract" purchasing. The supplier also benefits from decreased cost. Moreover, the supplier can obtain strategic leverage by creating increased revenue possibilities through tighter integration with buyers and lower selling costs.

For example, General Electric created a "Trading Process Network" that has turned a completely manual operation for custom-designed machine parts into an electronic system whereby requests for quotation, along with the required drawings, are sent out digitally to a global vendor base. Significant productivity increases, 50 percent cycle time reductions, lower materials acquisition costs, and lower overall materials costs are among the many benefits GE is realizing. Cisco Systems reduced acquisition costs by $105 per transaction through e-purchasing and process re-engineering.

The Mercer Consultants feel e-Purchasing provides organizations with the ability to automate routine practices and tighten supplier involvement and integration. However, world-class purchasing organizations are going beyond this. They are analyzing the more accurate and timely data that have become available in order to drive better purchasing, manufacturing, and design decisions. They are focusing on integrated supplier and vendor involvement, creative risk sharing, on-line auctions, complexity reduction, and management of complex channel relationships. e-Purchasing has provided the trigger for these initiatives.[14]

Evolving e-Commerce Technologies

Internet-based technologies become a very powerful tool at the buyer's disposal. The extent of this use will depend on the organization's resource commitment and the skill level of the purchasing personnel to adopt it. One technology that is always mentioned with the Internet is EDI. Some feel that EDI will disappear as an electronic technology while others feel it will remain a viable tool for purchasers. What appears more likely is that those EDI systems that evolve toward Internet-based technologies will survive and prosper while those that don't will experience a decrease in activity. These predictions will be discussed further in Chapter 3.

Purchasing cards may become one of the preferred payment methods for e-Purchasing. Systems-contracted items and vendor-managed-inventoried items may be bid out in Web-based auctions but deployed in the traditional way. Even the good old standard hard-copy purchase order may serve as the overriding set of terms and conditions that will be used to establish the framework for the agreement with the various Internet suppliers. Thus e-Purchasing will not totally replace traditional forms of business interaction but they will dramatically affect their use and modify how such processes are used.

Refinements in the status of e-Business and e-Purchasing systems is occurring daily and continually offering purchasers tailored solutions for their particular environments. Datasweep, Inc., based in San Jose, California, for example, has developed a "Webcentric" application to allow sales and marketing to track what is happening on the shop floor in build-to-order environments. The "Datasweep Advantage" allows companies to abandon paper-based tracking systems and pull down real-time information on production status, expected shipping date, and change-order feasibility through browser technology. The product integrates with ERP systems, and front-end order management tools are designed to move the manufacturing supply chain from informational Web sites to a virtual supply chain where sales, manufacturing, and materials-management are in sync.

One firm found that sales representatives were spending 20% of their time responding to customers' calls by having to go to the manufacturing floor to find out the status of particular jobs. The new Web-based software has reduced this type of tracking to 5% of their time. The company found it was now better able to schedule capacity, and it increased productivity by 25-30% through better control and fewer Interruptions.[15] Exhibit 1-4 shows the Dataquest vision of the evolution of the e-Commerce infrastructure.

Evolution of e-Commerce infrastructure

ERP ⟶ WWW ⟶ Web Orders ⟶ Web Service BTO ⟶
Mfg ⟶ Virtual Supply Chain

Source Datawseep, Inc.

Exhibit 1-4

Exhibit 1-4 shows how an organization might evolve in its ultimate quest to reach the *virtual supply chain*. First it puts an ERP system into place then starts using the Internet (WWW) to gather information about suppliers; then it starts placing orders on the Internet. Expanding the amount of business leads to a secure Internet or e-Commerce platform. It then begins to build to order as it can quickly please more customer wants and needs. Finally it adds the necessary communication software to enable it to get virtual information at any time and from any place on the supply chain. The improved communication capability and the ability to manage it provides the organization the flexibilty to manage inter and intra organizational linkages. These type linkages provide the ability to rapidly meet customer demands.

Putting New Zip Into Purchasing

Organizations implementing e-Purchasing report several benefits associated with cost reductions, productivity improvements, and consolidated servicing strategies. The first of these is cutting purchasing-transaction costs. Studies have shown that organizations can spend $75-$150 per order to procure all types of goods and services. These figures represent the organization's cost to place a purchase order and include both the hard-dollar costs of salaries, telephone and fax charges, order preparation, mailing, and order distribution costs and the soft-dollar costs such as the time the end-user spends to procure the good or service-supplier selection, expediting, etc.

When the dollar value of the order is low the cost to process an order often exceeds the value of the item or service being purchased or sold. From a pure transaction basis the number of small-dollar orders far exceed that of larger-dollar transactions in most organizations. Thus transaction costs are disproportionately high for low-value repetitive and non repetitive goods and services. The end result is that purchasers spending too much of their time on routine paperwork.

ProcureNet / Fisher Technology Group Case Example

A case example from Fisher Technologies Group illustrates the principle of high transaction costs. Cephalon, Inc., a rapidly growing biotechnology company, found that its purchase orders of less than $1,000 in value made up 70 percent of its paperwork processing load, yet represented less than 3 percent of the total purchasing dollars expended in a year. The company instituted Fisher's "Cornerstone" e-Purchasing system. Hard-dollar transaction costs dropped to $10 per purchase order since one-fourth of the transactions and the people required to process them were eliminated. And purchasing now spends less time approving low-value orders and more time on value-added activities like negotiating better deals with suppliers. Since more orders were placed with contracted suppliers, the company discovered that those suppliers were more willing to negotiate better deals. Savings of $25,000 here and $40,000 there were not uncommon, and the firm is continuing to pursue more opportunities.

Beyond the hard-cost savings, e-Purchasing solutions offer increased productivity and efficiencies by reducing the time end-users traditionally spent on activities like locating products in paper catalogs, completing requisition forms, checking product availability, obtaining price quotes, and getting approvals. Fisher Technologies estimates that their Web-based commerce solutions have allowed their clients to buy back, on average, 20 minutes of purchaser time per order. The result is that more time is spent on value-added activities like research and engineering, and less time on requisitioning supplies.

    Another hidden advantage is improved purchasing service to users. This benefit results in fewer salespeople calling on users to "sell" since they realize purchasing is in control and working with users to offer them multiple options in the e-purchasing system.(16)

Helping You Become an e-Purchaser

    This book is intended to provide the reader with an understanding of e-Purchasing as well as the tools necessary to implement the concepts within your organization through examples from other organizations and the authors' research and operating experiences. Section I which includes this chapter gives the reader an understanding of the e-Purchasing environment. In Chapter 2 the reader will gain an understanding of the Internet's development and associated terminology. Chapter 3 describes the typical purchasing process, how organizations have attempted to increase efficiencies, and the new business models which offer the potential to increase purchasing's strategic role.

    Section 2 enables the reader to grasp the key to making "e-Purchasing *plus*" a reality. Chapters 6 & 7 present key ideas to consider when starting an e-Purchasing program. In Chapters 8 & 9 you will begin to understand the how these concepts can be applied to both production and non-production buys. Chapter 10 provides helpful tips to ease the transition to an e-Purchasing program.

    Section 3 discusses the role of ERP in the overall e-Purchasing environment. The reader is exposed to the strengths and weaknesses of ERP installations in Chapters 11 & 12. Chapter 13 provides a description of useful sites for both ERP & Internet software providers. Finally, in Chapter 14 we take a look ahead and project what the "experts" think will happen to e-Purchasing in the context of the entire e-Commerce spectrum. The future is what you make of it and will to a large extent be dictated by the use of these wonderous technologies.

References

[1]Michael E. Porter, *Competitive Advantage* (New York: The Free Press, 1985).

[2]Steve Lohr, "Business to Business on the Internet", The New York Times, April 28, 1997, p. 1, 9.

[3]James Carbone, "Reinventing Purchasing Wins the Medal for Big Blue," Purchasing Magazine, September 16 1999, p. 38-66.

[4]Michael Dertouzos, What Will Be: How the New World of Information Will Change our Lives (New York: Harper Rowe), 1997.

[5]Ward Hanson, *Principles of Internet Marketing* (Cincinnati: Southwestern Publishing, 2000), p. 3.

[6]Gary McWilliams and Joseph B. White, "Dell to Detroit: Get into Gear," Wall Street Journal, December 1, 1999, p. B1, B4).

[7]WSJ, December 1, 1999.

[8]WSJ, December 1, 1999.

[9]WSJ, December 1, 1999.

[10]Gregory White, "How GM and Ford Think Web Can Make Splash On the Factory Floor," Wall Street Journal, December 3, 1999, p. 1,8.

[11]WSJ, December 3, 1999.

[12]W. D. Perrault and E. Jerome McCarthy, Basic Marketing: R.D. Irwin. 1996, p. 429-433, Homewood, IL.

[13] John Evan Brook; http://pubs.cmpnet.com

[14]Craig DeLano and Rex Tibbens, "Is an E-Purchasing Solution Right for You?" June 1, 1999, Mercer Management Consulting (on line). Available from http://www.purchasingcenter.com

[15]Jennifer L. Baljko, "Datasweep Offers Advantage to Manufacturers," in Electronic Buyers News, September 27, 1999, p. 86.

[16]Barbara Pearson, "Electronic Purchasing: A Case History", Fisher Technology Group, Pittsburgh, PA, 1997.

2
Evolution
of the Internet

What is the World Wide Web?

For years people have dreamed about the concept of a universal information database. This data would be accessible to people around the world, and information would link easily to other pieces of information so that only the most important data would be found quickly by a user. The idea of global data was first explored in the 1960s and spawned the idea of a universal document that would revolutionize all aspects of human information interaction.

In the 1990s technology caught up with these dreams and made possible the implementation of this concept worldwide. One description of the World Wide Web is as a "wide-area hypermedia information-retrieval initiative aiming to give universal access to a large universe of documents." Essentially the Web makes information available to users who are connected by a series of networks. Therefore it is popular to describe the Internet as a massive worldwide series of connected computers giving and receiving information. The Internet is comprised of thousands of smaller regional networks scattered throughout the globe.

Web Terminology

Many sources, including this book, use the terms World Wide Web and Internet interchangeably. Technically the *World Wide Web* is the body of information, while the Internet refers to the physical side of the network and includes the computers and connections on the network. The Internet can also be viewed as the sum total of devices interconnected using the *Internet Protocol (IP)*. The IP is an open communication network that allows computers to interconnect with each other through "*client-server*" networks. The major client-server system is known as the World Wide Web (Web).

The Web works under the client-server model. The Web "*server*" is a program running on a computer whose only purpose is to serve documents to other computers when asked to. A Web "*client*" is a program that interfaces with the user and requests documents from the server as the user asks for them.

The standard language that the Web uses for creating and recognizing hypermedia documents, and that Web clients and servers use to communicate with each other, is called the "*HyperText Transmission Protocol*" (HTTP). All Web clients and servers must be able to "speak" HTTP in order to send and receive hypermedia documents. Thus Web servers are often called HTTP servers. A "Web browser" such as Netscape's Navigator or Microsoft's Internet Explorer are clients used to request a specific HTTP page.

Hypertext is very similar to regular text in that it can be stored, read, searched, or edited. What separates hypertext from normal text is that it contains connections to other documents. The text that has links to other documents is termed "*hyper links*" text. Hypertext that contains links to other forms of media such as sounds, images, and movies is termed "hypermedia." For example, if you see a product you like and click on a hyper link, you will be directed to a two-minute verbal description of the product's characteristics.

The person given credit for creating the Web was Tim

Berners-Lee, who created the uniform resource locator (URL) as the way to specify an address on the Web. Berners-Lee also invented the hypertext markup language (HTML), which is used to create Web pages. *Mosaic*, developed by Marc Andreesen, is a browser allowing graphical interface on personal computers (PCs). The combination of the Web and Mosaic standardized and simplified the way in which the Internet could be accessed and allowed for its tremendous growth, which continues today. For example, a popular Web site for purchasers is *www.napm.org*, which provides a wealth of information about the educational opportunities, activities, and resources in the purchasing area.[1]

Brief History of the Internet

The seed for what would later be known as the Internet was planted in about 1945, when President Roosevelt's science advisor, Vannevar Bush, proposed a conceptual machine, called MEMEX, that could store vast amounts of information. MEMEX gave users the ability to create information trails, such as links of related text and illustrations, which could then be stored and used for future reference.

It wasn't until 1968 that the US Government--specifically the Department of Defense (DOD)--stepped up its interest in computer communications. Prompted by Cold War paranoia and the fear that a possible thermonuclear attack by the Soviet Union might end the military's ability to transfer information across America, the DOD began funding research on computer networking for military communications. Its goal was to create a computer network that could sustain partial destruction in case of an attack and still function as a network.

The DOD developed a system in which computers could communicate directly with each other, rather than depending solely on a "hub," or main computer, for information. And in 1969, DOD workers began operating a nuclear war-proof information/communication network called the Advanced Research Project Agency

Network (ARPANET).

When the ARPANET first went on line, it had only four sites--all located on the campuses of the University of California--which interconnected the computers of several government scientists and defense contractors. The traffic in the network was mostly text messages sent by e-mail. The information could travel via alternate routes, as opposed to along a single fixed path, so that if one computer malfunctioned, other computers could detour around the problem and keep information moving.

During this time, computer technology consisted of expensive, large-scale mainframes and minicomputers used by governments, institutions, and corporations. But in 1971, shortly after the launch of ARPANET, the first microprocessor was invented. It had the capability to do the work of several single-silicon chips. Smaller than a postage stamp, it contained as much power as the first electronic computer, which was so large it filled an entire room.

The following year would see two major breakthroughs: the introduction of Telnet, which made it easier for a computer to connect to a remote (host) computer, and the addition of several more universities to the network, bringing the total number of connected universities and military sites to fifty.

The ARPANET, which had become known as the "Internet," continued to grow; by 1975 it spanned the entire globe. The same year, the first home desktop computer, the Altair 8800, was introduced.

By 1978, the Internet was no longer restricted to the Department of Defense, and channels became available for academic communications through USENET News. The following year saw the creation of CompuServe, a consumer-oriented on-line service, and IBM introduced its version of the personal computer (PC) in 1981.

In the late 1980s there were about 80,000 computers on the Internet. But although the Internet was in place, there was really no way to browse it. There were no colorful pictures or icons for easy reference, so if a person wanted to navigate through the Net, he had to have technical knowledge of the interconnected computers. But in 1989, British researcher Tim Berners-Lee (as discussed previously) came up with the idea of connecting electronic documents around the globe for easy access: his World Wide Web (WWW) became available to the public in 1992. The first Web browser, Mosaic 1.0, was released in 1993, and by the end of the year there were several browsers to choose from.[2]

Internet Security

Anyone who has ever bought, sold, or provided information via the Internet understands concerns about security. This concern extends to various databases and specifications inside the purchaser's organization. Security in the design and operation of computer and database-management systems requires a cooperative effort of both developers and users to ensure the integrity of the systems and the confidentiality of data and information. The three levels of security are 1) physical access, meaning the limits in personal contact with the equipment and stored data, 2) password access, which includes limiting transaction use or information viewing to only those authorized to do so, and 3) internal protection, which includes programs designed to maintain system integrity such as virus protection.

Four of the more common security techniques are 1) fire walls, 2) encryption, 3) data backup, and 4) digital or electronic signatures. A fire wall is a computer system that sits between the server and the rest of the Internet. The fire-wall software is programmed to decide what kinds of information are allowed to move between the particular site and the outside environment. Encryption is another security measure, which involves the coding of sensitive data that can be decoded only by software available to authorized users. (The encryption technology uses the public-key system, which is covered under the electronic signatures section below).

Backups of data procedures ensure the security of data in the event of system problems, crashes, or viruses. Software manufacturers also provide procedures to recover lost data files in their programs. Digital/Electronic signatures are short units of data bearing mathematical relationships to the data in the document's content and are transmitted using public-key cryptography programs. These programs create a pair of keys (one public key and one private key), and what the public key encrypts, only the private key can decrypt. Alternatively, what the private key encrypts, only the public key can decrypt. This assures confidentiality if information, and the digital signature allows the receiver to verify the identity of the sender of the data.[3]

Information Technology Basics[*]

Knowledge of computer hardware/software terminology is an important building block for the e-Purchaser. It is imperative that the purchasing professional be aware of the most common computer terms and related expressions. Such knowledge will enable the purchaser to interface intelligently with hardware and software suppliers, as well as internal departments, with regard to the acquiring, using, and maintaining of computer equipment and systems. Finally, this knowledge will help select and run the best systems within the purchasing department.

The following terminology reflects some of what is currently applicable to purchasing and supply-management environments. *Data* represent the basic facts and figures that constitute inputs to the computer. *Information* is those results derived from the data that have been processed by the computer into a more useful output, which can then be used within the organization to make better decisions. A *record* is a series of related data elements such as a single supplier's company name and primary contact. It is important to separate records so they can be used by more than one file. A *file* is a set of related records that contain data about an entry. For example, a supplier file would contain the supplier's company name, address, phone number, and e-mail address. A *digital system* is a computer

---

[*]Much of the following is taken from Giunipero's work on the *C.P.M. Study Guide* 7th edition.

system that uses the binary digits (0 and 1) to represent data. A *bit* is the smallest amount of data and is one binary digit. A byte is a group of 8 bits and is also termed a character.

Hardware refers to the physical part of an information system. Hardware provides the means by which a user can access the computer system and has various components, including devices for input, processing, storage, and output. Examples of hardware include computer terminals, networks, scanners, and printers.

Input devices are physical items and include keyboards, touch screens, scanners, voice recognition instruments, and readers of magnetically coded tape or disk drives. Some of these devices will also operate as output devices. The *Central Processing Unit (CPU)* is the centerpiece of the computer system or, strictly speaking, the computer itself. It is composed of the control unit (which decodes program instructions and directs other components of the computer to perform the task specified in the program instructions), the arithmetic-logic unit (which does multiplication, division, subtraction, and addition; and compares the relative magnitude of two pieces of data) and the primary storage unit (which stores program instructions currently being executed and stores data while they are being processed by the CPU).

Storage refers to media used for both the short- and long-term storage of data and includes mass storage devices, tape, and discs. Hard or fixed discs provide room for storing large amounts of data that can be retrieved quickly, but they lack mobility. *Floppy discs* provide an easy, portable way to store data, but space is limited and they can be damaged or lost. Removable disc cartridges (such as Zip drives) combine the storage capacity of a hard disk with portability. *CD-ROMs* are becoming a common way to store programs, and some have writable capabilities. *Digital Video Disk (DVD)* technology provides enhanced quality and faster retrieval of video images than traditional tape. Diskpacs and magnetic tape are reliable and inexpensive but can be accessed only sequentially. *Mass-storage devices* have very large capacities as well as automated access and retrieval capabilities. The process of retrieving the tape and copying it to magnetic disc, however, is slow.

Output devices include magnetic tapes and disks, printers, laser imaging devices, computer-output microfiche (COM) cards, voice-output devices, and terminals. Some of these devices will also operate as input devices. *Microcomputers* are associated with *Personal Computers (PCs),* which represent the microcomputer category today. Rapid advances in technology have provided increased computing power in smaller devices at lower prices. PCs are available in desktop, laptop, and palm-held models. The latter two are popular because of their portability. *Modems* (modulators/demodulators) are devices used for converting data into formats for transmission over telephone and cable lines and then converting them back again for computer use. Modem capabilities are expressed in "baud" rates, which means bytes per second (bps) or the speed at which data can be transmitted.

Software is a set of instructions for a particular application (run) or the performance of a specific task that the computer will execute with accuracy and reliability. It is essentially the perceived or actual capability to mimic human decision-making and the processing of data or information. The major types of software are discussed in a later section. Software can be acquired off-the-shelf, developed in-house, or outsourced.

Off-the-shelf software refers to standard versions that are commercially available and require no modification. They are ready to run and install right out of the box. Most personal computer software is off-the-shelf. Most standard applications lend themselves to off-the-shelf software.

In-house software is developed by the organization's Information Services (IS) department personnel for cases when users require software applications that are unique and don't exist off the shelf. Outsourcing software involves contracting with a software supplier or third party to develop a software package. If the organization lacks in-house capabilities, expertise, or time, outsourcing provides an attractive alternative. Correctly outsourcing software development requires consideration of a range of alternatives, from having the supplier modify an existing package to having a third party develop a completely new system.

Software engineering is a process whereby individuals design, structure, and document software. To assure product quality, extensive simulation tests are performed prior to product release. The Software Engineering Institute is a federally funded research and development center located at Carnegie Mellon University. The center was established by Congress to address the transition of software-engineering technology. The goal of the Institute is to improve the quality of systems that depend on software.

Management Information System (MIS) refers to a system for providing information used for decision-making. Processing refers to the transformation of data into accurate and meaningful information. Real-time on-line processing handles transactions at the time they occur and provides output directly to users. It avoids the delays and provides users complete and up-to-date information. *Batch processing* is a system whereby data are collected and processed in groups. It is used for large amounts of data that are processed on a set schedule such as Supplier Performance Ratings.

Distributed Data Processing refers to a system in which data resources are accessible at many locations. The user has access to data regardless of his/her location. Data can be stored at several locations that are connected by a data-communications network of terminals and computers that interface via phone or cable lines. If a centralized mainframe is used for this type of processing, the organization usually will have a central data processing center where documents are sent for data entry and then distributed to user sites.

Decision support systems (DSS) help users make better business decisions through the analysis of external and internal data. Such systems allow the user to create a model of the critical factors affecting a decision and pose "what if" questions by changing the variables. Negotiation support systems (NSS) are a subset or type of DSS system in that they permit the user to simulate potential outcomes based on each party's wants and needs. They also may suggest certain strategies that the purchaser could use in the negotiation. Users must remember that these support systems are only tools and not replacements for good human judgment and analysis.

Hardware Types and Configurations

Recent advances in computer technology have diluted the categorization of computer hardware. Applications that required the power of a mainframe computer 20 years ago can now easily be performed on a personal computer. The three traditional classes of computers are microcomputers (PCs), minicomputers (small-scale), and mainframe (large-scale) computers.

Personal computers are the backbone of most individual and systems-computing needs. Each is run by a powerful microprocessor that holds the arithmetic and logic and registers and controls all functions and calculations. *Minicomputers* are medium-scale systems that function as multi-user systems for several hundred users. Today *mid-range computer* and server are more popular terms for minicomputer or mid-sized systems. Mainframe computers are very powerful machines that run large-scale applications requiring a large amount of memory and storage capacity. There are small, medium, and large-scale mainframes, handling from a handful to tens of thousands of on-line terminals. Large-scale mainframes support multiple gigabytes of main memory and terabytes of disk storage. Large mainframes use smaller computers as front-end processors that connect to the communications networks.

Computer Workstation is a phrase that has many different meanings. First, it can represent a high-performance, single-user microcomputer or minicomputer that is used for graphics, CAD, CAE, simulation, and scientific applications. It is typically an RISC-based computer that runs under some variation of UNIX. High-end Pentium PCs now compete with workstations in performance. Second, a personal computer in a network is considered a workstation. Third, in the telecommunications industry it means a combined telephone and computer. Finally, a terminal or personal computer can be considered a workstation.

Client-server configurations is a phrase most often used in conjunction with networking. A computer network is a group of physically connected computers (or workstations) that are attached to a file server. Networking allows users to share software and some hardware, thus reducing costs while providing the user more applications. A network administrator is a user who is assigned to manage all aspects of the network, such as adding new users, assigning security levels, and managing print queues.

Local Area Network (LAN) describes an interconnection of a group of personal computers and terminals within a defined area or location such as a department or office. The server permits a sharing of software and information between multiple users. This system's architecture is referred to as a "client server" system. A *wide area network (WAN)* is an interconnection of personal computers and/or LANs across a business unit, division, or company on a worldwide basis. The communication interface is accomplished via use of fibre optic cables, phone lines, or satellites. Some people today refer to these WANs as intranets.

Systems software is a set of programs that controls the use of the hardware and software resources, and that allocates computer-system resources to application programs based on their needs or priorities. Examples are MS-DOS, OS/2, and MAC-OS. Application software is a program written for or by a user that processes data to produce information needed by users. The three major types of applications software are word processors, databases, and spreadsheets. Programming languages such as C++, Java, Basic, FOR-TRAN, and COBOL are used for establishing specialized applications when no off-the-shelf application package is available. Network software is any software package that supports networking capabilities for LANs and WANs.

Uses of Computer Hardware/Software

The computer has become a standard tool for decision-making and information dissemination in all organizations. Applications for each type of computer continue to grow in number and scope. The following are general computer applications used in organizations. *Word processing* is used for the creation, modification, and editing of text material in various formats. It allows the user to create quality documents, reports, summaries, tables, forms, and graphic presentations. *Desktop publishing* is a form of word processing that uses an applications software package to make printed matter more attractive and effective. It combines text and graphics data for the production of "professional looking" publications without resorting to more traditional printing methodologies.

Spreadsheets are programs that permit the management and analysis of numerical data and that organize such data in graphs and charts for presentations and reports. Database management allows the user to manage data observations and events. Analysis is accomplished by aggregating or separating this data into a logical format for specific applications and information requirements. Forecasting and modeling data and information are secured from previously acquired data-processing operations and manipulated by an application-software process for output into reports or displays. Such output is utilized as a decision support tool for management.

Modeling may represent the use of *Computer Aided Design (CAD)* in its interface with numerically controlled machines, and *Computer Aided Manufacturing (CAM)* in its control of machine centers and industrial robots. In addition, modeling may take the form of "what if" analysis in both fiscal and manufacturing applications. "What if" analysis is also referred to as simulation. Graphics/drawing applications are utilized with the various types of computers to offer illustrations of numerical data for decision-making and information-dissemination purposes. Various software products are acquired or created for this purpose.

Electronic mail (E-mail) is the transmission of memos and messages over a network. Within an organization, users can send mail to a single or multiple user(s). With multi-tasking workstations, mail can be delivered and announced while the user is working in an application. Otherwise, mail is sent to a simulated mailbox in the network server or host computer, which must be interrogated. An e-mail system requires a messaging system, which provides the store and forward capabilities, and a mail program that provides the user interface with send and receive functions. The Internet transformed e-mail into one global system from separate, isolated entities.[4]

Computers Help Purchasing

Applying a computer system to purchasing and supply management allows the purchasing professional to concentrate on non-clerical duties and responsibilities. Typical applications include database management systems (DBMS), which allow for management of wide arrays of data records. The relationship between two specific records is called a "*set.*" *Relational databases* have data organized in two-dimensional tables. Each row is an attribute (e.g., a specific person's name) and each column is a field (e.g., name). *Object-oriented* systems focus on the data, not the process. The data are then accessed in the form users request through an "object library."

Typical files used in purchasing that become part of a DBMS include supplier files, purchase order/requisition files, price files, follow-up/expediting files, delivery/return files, acknowledgments, purchase records, commodity files, and files of contracts. Each organization will use any or all of these data sources to accommodate its records and documentation needs.[5]

Database Applications in Purchasing

Performance-measurement (e.g., supplier) *software* programs provide for the compilation and recording of key data to permit the evaluation of supplier performance on quality, delivery, and price. These reports can be forwarded electronically, with improvement suggestions, on a periodic basis to suppliers for their review and response. The system provides for the timely collection of data-instant compilation. Therefore much data about supplier performance that were either too time consuming to capture or too detailed to analyze are now available.

Project-management software programs provide the ability to plan, estimate, execute, and monitor individual projects such as construction of new facilities, development of new products, etc. *Analytical applications software* in Purchasing/Supply Management provides analytical analysis of several important decisions. The functions this software is used for include bid analysis; make, buy, or outsource decisions; leasing alternatives; and optimum order quantities. Transactional uses for computer systems and software programs allow for increased efficiency in processing requests for quotations, material releases, purchase orders, change notices, etc.

Cost-data-management software permits the tracking of internal costs and personnel costs; supplier cost data also can be collected and compared to indices such as the Producer Price Index. Asset management is the accounting of the original book cost of assets (buildings and equipment), as well as the accumulated depreciation, location, and condition of physical assets. In the event of an emergency such costs provide invaluable assistance in settling insurance claims.

Enterprise Software

Enterprise software is popularly termed *Enterprise Resource Planning (ERP)*. ERP is an integrated information system that serves all departments within an enterprise. Such programs are usually modularly packaged software programs, and these modules may be able to interface with an organization's own software with varying degrees of effort. Depending on the vendor, ERP software also may be alterable via programming. An ERP system can include software for manufacturing, order entry, accounts receivable and payable, general ledgers, purchasing, warehousing, transportation, and human resources. (See Chapter 4 for more discussion or ERP.)

Material Requirements Planning (MRP) is a powerful set of software programs that provide for the management of inventory through interactions with purchasing, marketing, and operations.

MRP became popular as a way to control inventories in the late 1970s, when computing power finally was able to support the lengthy and frequent calculations required to keep schedule priorities current. It is based on the premise that demand for component inventory of a manufactured product is dependent on the sales of the finished product. The computer continually regenerates schedules and the updated priorities. Proper use of MRP systems has resulted in an increased ability to control inventory and better schedule suppliers.

Firms found the data in MRP systems so useful that they decided it would be good to use the MRP data to assist with financial and strategic planning. Thus the term *MRP II* was coined to add financial, strategic, and capacity planning. Designers envisioned MRP II as a tool to enable a firm to develop and monitor its strategic plans and goals.

Distribution Requirements Planning (DRP) was another step in the evolution of the MRP concept. DRP extended the dependent demand concepts forward in the supply chain to help organizations better plan and control inventory at their distributors. DRP systems were particularly suited to firms with extensive distributor networks such as pharmaceuticals and food companies. Finally, as previously mentioned above, the 1990s brought ERP systems. These systems could be considered an extension of the MRPII concept but with much more power. The goal of ERP is to have one system that enables management to better run all the functions in the entire enterprise.

Electronic Data Interchange

Electronic data interchange (EDI) is a computer application that has been used by purchasers to conduct business electronically for the past 10 years. Providers of this technology have realized the need to adapt quickly or lose business to the Internet-based systems; some are using the Internet to supplement their technologies. EDI is the computer-to-computer transfer of documentation and information between organizations. The purpose of EDI is to allow for data and documentation to be directly processed and acted upon by the receivers. EDI is the inter-corporate electronic transfer of common business forms such as releases, purchase orders, invoices, and shipping notices.

The three major categories of EDI systems are: 1) One-to-many, wherein a single company buys from numerous suppliers directly connected to that organization; 2) Value-added networks (VAN), which are electronic warehouses or depositories into which transmissions are stored and then transferred to the appropriate party electronically (VANs permit easy buyer and seller interactions); and 3) Third-party networks, which permit a buyer's computer to interface with a number of suppliers' computers in any format, greatly expanding the choice of suppliers and commodities. Such a network operates as a central communications switch. It receives a company's purchase orders in a batch, separates them by supplier, holds those for each supplier in an electronic mailbox, and then transmits the orders to the suppliers at predetermined times. The suppliers then process the data and ship the buyers' requirements.

The advantages of EDI are numerous and similar to those associated with buying over the Internet. The most immediate benefit of EDI is the reduction of paperwork necessary to complete transactions; it also allows for improved accuracy, reduced clerical work, reduced order-cycle time, and increased productivity. Longer-term benefits, as a result of the reduction of paperwork, also include additional time for buyers to conduct other analytical activities.

The fact that EDI enhances productivity makes it unnecessary to hire additional personnel. EDI also fosters the development of integrated and improved purchasing and supply-chain systems by encouraging the use of complimentary technologies such as JIT bar coding and Electronic Funds Transfer. Buyers act as commodity managers, focusing on managing a smaller number of suppliers in order to reduce the total costs of doing business.

EDI has an advantage over Internet purchasing in at least one area--standards. Several organizations, notably the American

National Standards Institute (ANSI), have produced standards suitable for a wide range of purchasing transactions. The ANSI X12
standards are applicable to almost any form of purchase order, and
to other documents such as invoices, shipping notices, freight bills,
and acknowledgments. The use of ANSI X12 standards has resulted
in the rapid growth of EDI. The National Association of Purchasing
Management supports the adoption of the ANSI X12 standards to
facilitate company-to-company electronic communications.

The steps in EDI implementation for most organizations
would include the following:

1.) Establish a need for EDI.
2.) Establish a planning committee.
3.) Perform an EDI audit to assess current status, availability
   of information systems resources, and level of interest of
   personnel. Availability of standards and current practices
   of trading partners and competitors, as well as availability of support from third-party networks, should also
   be considered.
4.) Present a plan of action to top management and directors.
5.) Decide on a type of system. This will include a decision
   on types of standards, system configuration, and third-
   party networks. The suppliers to be used should also be
   selected at this point.
6.) Provide education for potential users and suppliers.
7.) Present final plan and pilot test schedule to top manage
   ment for approval.
8.) Establish contact with trading partners.
9.) Conduct pilot test of system.
10.) Evaluate the system.
11.) Expand system on an incremental basis.

Since EDI precludes the use of signed contracts, a separate
contract governing the terms and conditions associated with doing
business using EDI must be established. In general, such contracts

should state that purchase orders will be transmitted electronically and that the buyers and sellers authorize third-party networks to share data. The contract should also state the designated locations for scheduled deliveries, and that functional acknowledgments of transmitted documents should be sent.[6]

e-Purchasing Systems

e-Purchasing is similar to EDI in that it involves the computer-to-computer transfer of information. It involves doing business on line, typically via the Web. It has alternately been called e-business and e-commerce (as mentioned in Chapter 1), could refer to electronic data interchange (EDI). One of the major advantages E-commerce over EDI is its relatively low cost. One source estimated that the costs for private VANs in EDI systems are approximately $150 per hour.

There are currently three major types of e-commerce systems. They are the sell-side systems, buy-side systems, and third-party systems. Each system has its own advantages and disadvantages, which are discussed in detail in Chapter 3.

Electronic Funds Transfer (EFT) is the transfer of funds electronically from one computer to another. This process saves organizations the processing costs associated with the payment cycle such as invoicing, check generation, mailing, and depositing.

Intranets and Extranets

The intranet is an in-house Web site that serves the employees of the enterprise. Although intranet pages may link to the Internet, an intranet is not a site accessed by the general public. Intranets use the same communications protocols and hypertext links as the Web and thus provide a standard way of disseminating information internally and extending the application worldwide at the same time

The extranet is a Web site for existing customers and suppliers as opposed to the general public. It can provide access to suppli-

er-design information, current inventories, and internal databases--
virtually any information that is private and not published for everyone. An extranet uses the public Internet as its transmission system,
but requires passwords to gain access. (See Chapter 3 for additional
discussions.)

Russell Corporation's Extranet

Russell Corporation, an Alexander, Ala.-based manufacturer
of athletic apparel, wanted to make sure that its extranet helped its
customers make it easier to do business with its customers so it
named its extranet project "Customer Outreach."

Customer Outreach now brings business data to 35 (soon to
be expanded to 60) authorized Russell distributors in the United
States through an Internet link supplied by DeltaCom. The customers' point of access is a Web server outside the company's fire
wall that runs an Internet Information Server. It passes formatted
database queries through a fire wall to a universal database running
on a Windows NT server.

To provide Russell's business partners with current, accurate
information about their accounts, that database is constantly updated
with downloads from the firm's DB2 operational databases, which
run on a mainframe computer. The Customer Outreach Extranet
went into production in January 1998, after four months of design
and two months of beta testing.

There would have been no point to the extranet if it didn't
supply the information customers wanted. Russell involved their
sales force in creating a customer group of distributors. Surveys of
the group revealed the top 10 pieces of information that customers
wanted on line. Though extranets provide many benefits, the main
advantages are better customer service and lower costs (made possible by customer self-service and support), according to the Gartner
Group, a consulting firm. Customer representatives don't have to
spend as much time answering basic questions about transactions
and orders, since customers can get this information themselves

from the extranet. Customer representatives now spend their time solving problems and helping customers and partners make better decisions.

Barry Hall, a principal at the San Francisco office of consultancy Coopers & Lybrand, notes that an extranet not only does the right things, it does the right things for the right people. "It puts information in the hands of those who need it when they need it," he explains. In fact, once companies are interconnected, an extranet can broaden everyone's horizons, sometimes in unconventional ways.

Distributors for SilverPlatter Information of Norwood, Mass., are also pleased with the ability to conduct transactions electronically. Approximately 100 customers of this publisher of CD-ROM bibliographic databases do business over its extranet. Users from Europe, Asia, Africa, and the Americas can find out when their subscriptions expire, check on pricing, and determine when an order will be shipped.

"Because of time-zone differences, some of our customers simply cannot call during our normal business hours," explains senior developer Tom Bergman. "In addition, our prices are complex and constantly changing. The extranet has solved these problems. It allows us to conduct business without regard to time zones and geography, and to build a truly borderless business environment." The extranet is powered by a server running an Internet Information Server. SilverPlatter used Progress Software's WebSpeed to build the site, which has access to SilverPlatter's operational databases, also from Progress Software. The company connects to the Internet via two T1 lines from GTE Inter networking and UUNet.[3]

File Transfer Protocol (FTP) is a protocol used to transfer files over a network such as the Internet and UNIX. It includes functions to log onto the network, list directories, and copy files. It can also convert between the ASCII and EBCDIC character codes. FTP operations can be performed by typing commands at a command prompt. FTP transfers can also be initiated from within a Web browser by entering the URL preceded with ftp://. Unlike e-mail programs to which graphics and program files have to be "attached," FTP is designed to handle binary files directly and does not add the overhead of encoding and decoding the data.[7]

e-Purchasing Training

Ultimately, the success of any new system depends on the skills of the people who operate and use it. Purchasing personnel should be familiar with the various applications of the computer technology, e-purchasing terminology, and theory.

Training should be focused on the use of both hardware and software in specific execution of conducting business electronically. E-purchasing is tool for helping the purchaser make better decisions and become more strategic in decision making and information dissemination. This technology needs to be integrated in his daily routines to assist in the various aspects of his individual responsibilities. Training may be available from both internal and external sources, and management may decide the appropriate use of these sources based on fiscal, time, and policy/procedural constraints.

The development and conducting of in-house training about a software package or new hardware is usually a joint project involving purchasing and the Information Systems department. Such joint development for training is particularly common when the software is developed specifically for a purchasing application.

It is common to outsource training in cases where the software is purchased or modified. The major reason for this is that the software provider is an expert on its system and has the staff available to perform this training. During the negotiation phase of the software acquisition process, it is common to request training as part of the package. In some cases suppliers will offer a set amount of training free of charge. In other cases the extent and cost of training is negotiable.[8]

References

[1]Kevin Hughes, "Entering the World Wide Web: A Guide to Cyberspace," available from www.hcc.hawaii.edu/guide/, October, 1993.

[2]"Internet 101," in Ideas for Investors (Prudential Securities, February 1999).

[3]Charles F. Hofacker, Internet Marketing (Digital Springs, Texas: Digital Springs Publishing, 1999), p. 164.

[4]E. Muller and Allen Raedels, *C.P.M. Study Guide* , 7th edition, Forthcoming 2000, (Tempe, AZ: NAPM).

[5]Gary Shelly, T. Cashman, and H. Rosenblatt, Systems Analysis and Design (Cambridge, MA: Course Technology, 1998).

[6][4]E. Muller and Allen Raedels, *C.P.M. Study Guide* , 7th edition, Forthcoming 2000, (Tempe, AZ: NAPM).

[7]Samuel Greengard, "Extranets: The e-business Link," Beyond Computing, Vol. 7, No. 5 (June 1998).

[8]Brian Caffrey, D. Steggell, and R. Weissman, "Electronic Commerce: Your Tool to Value-added Purchasing and Supply Management, NAPM Info Edge", February 1998, Vol 3, No. 6, p. 16.

3
Purchasing's System Evolution

Purchasing -- a Transaction-Intensive Function

The purchasing function, like other transaction-intensive functions in an organization, has continually needed streamlining and improvement in order to make both it and the organization more efficient and effective. An analysis of the typical business cycle provides an idea of how *transaction-intensive* the purchasing function is.

The business cycle starts with a sales order or a customer purchase order. The order-entry group then enters this sales order and combines with other orders into a schedule, which is then translated into requirements. The actual items on the schedule and its quality of requirements are either purchased or built in-house. Regardless of whether the items are purchased or built, some purchasing action is required through interaction with suppliers. Purchase orders are issued, ship dates are established with suppliers, and transportation firms are selected. This process generates several different documents and is paperwork intensive. Once the shipment is received, shipping reports, inspection reports, and stock level status updates are issued. These internal documents generate more paperwork.

As the order goes through the operations process, customer service often initiates order tracking to provide the customer with up-to-date status reports. Once the operations process is completed, shipping documents are prepared, along with bills of lading, customer packing slips, and invoices.

This example illustrates the transaction intensity required to satisfy a customer order. Exhibit 3-1 shows this process and how purchasing is directly or indirectly involved in a multiple number of these transactions. It is important to remember that the direct requirements from customer orders are only part of purchasing's transaction load. The other part of the load is generated by functions that support the order-fulfillment process. These functions, which include maintenance, engineering, research, administrative support, disposal, and scrap/surplus sales, all generate a significant transaction load for the purchasing department.

Exhibit 3-1, Typical Business Transaction Cycle

Activity	Primary Document(s)
Customer Order	Sales Order & Customer Purchase Order
Order Entry/Customer Service	Customer Order & Customer Change Order
Operations Planning	Bill of Materials & Requirements List
Production Planning	Inventory, Storeroom, Purchase Requisition

Exhibit 3-1continued

Purchasing	Purchase Requisitio, Purchase Order & Change Order
Purchasing (indirect)	Purchase Requisition & Order & Change Order

(Support Groups for indirect buyers are maintenance, engineering, research and development)

Supplier	Purchase Order, Acknowledgment, Invoice Packing Slip, Bill of Lading
Incoming Transportation	Bill of Lading, Packing Slip
Receiving	Receiving Report
Incoming Inspection	Inspection Report, Return Material for Rejection
Storeroom	Stores Report, Inventory Report
Build Schedule	Order Release Form, Kitting Form
Shipping	Bill of Lading
Outbound Transportation	Customer Packing Slip
Accounts Payable	Invoice Processing and Debits
Accounts Receivable	Customer Billing/Customer Payment Process
Disposal & Surplus Sales	Contracts and Shipments
Hazardous Waste Disposal	Contracts and Manifests and Bill of Lading

Changing the Traditional Business Cycle

Cisco Systems, one of the leading network systems providers, has used electronic commerce to change its business model. The traditional way business was conducted at Cisco involved the customer filling out a purchase request form and faxing it to Cisco. At Cisco an employee typed the information into the company's order system. Other employees, using this internal system, then confirmed the accuracy of the customer information and scheduled manufacturing for the requested products. Purchasing would get involved with the faxing or sending out of purchase orders to suppliers. Cisco calculated that one out of every four times, the forms had enough mistakes that the customer had to start the process again.

In the *new method* the customer goes to the Cisco Web site and enters the purchase request onto an electronic page. The on-line order form is rejected by screening software if there is a problem, so the customer can correct it immediately. The completed request goes directly into an order database, which allows production scheduling to be handled electronically. Cisco estimates that the time from order entry to production has been cut in half.

Customer Service and Support has also been changed by the electronic business approach. Under the old system a customer called to check the status of an order, request service, or ask for a software upgrade. A customer-service agent logged onto Cisco's internal computer system and checked the status of the order, requested service, or asked for a software upgrade. New software was mailed to customers on computer disks.

Under the new customer-service model, those certified customers with passwords get direct access to the computer systems that monitor Cisco's operations. These customers can check the status of orders, find answers to technical questions, and download new software. There is also an on-line self-help section for customers; Cisco estimates that this section alone averts 250,000 phone calls a month.

The benefit to Cisco customers like Jason Valore, a buyer for Comstor Innovative Distribution Services, which designs and installs computer networks, is faster, more accurate orders. That translates to better service to Comstor's own Customers.[1]

The Purchase-Order Cycle

Over time purchasers have developed systems to handle the transaction load more efficiently since (as discussed in Chapter 1) the typical cost of preparing and processing one purchase order ranges from $75 to $200. Part of the reason for such costs are the various touch points in the process. As is shown is EXHIBIT 3-2 there are not only several steps in the process, but several steps when costs are incurred and several copies of paperwork generated.

Exhibit 3-2, Typical Purchase-Order Cycle

1. Requisitioner/User Requisition
2. Approval
3. Requisition to Purchasing
4. Sourced, Priced, Scheduled
5. Purchase Order Generated (7 copies)
6. Mailed to Supplier
7. Supplier returns acknowledgment
8. Supplier Ships
9. Items Received
10. Inspected
11. Stores/User
12. Invoice Matched
13. Invoice Paid
14. Disposal of Excess

Paper-Based Efficiency Systems

To reduce these purchasing costs and lengthy cycle times,

and to fill user requests more quickly, purchasers over the years have developed several systems to streamline this traditional process and cut the cost involved with the transaction. This was particularly necessary for items that were low in dollar value and/or for non-repetitive-type purchases. Some of the first approaches involved *Cash on Delivery (C.O.D.)*, in which the purchasing firm maintained a petty cash account and paid for small purchases in cash. Using *telephone ordering systems* was another approach whereby the purchase requisition was phoned in by the buyer and a copy sent to receiving. The supplier received no paperwork under this system, but shipped the goods in good faith; once the material was received it was paid for by matching the receiving report to the supplier's invoice.

Under the *Purchase Order Draft system*, the supplier would receive a check with the order, thus totally eliminating the need for invoicing. This system held a lot of promise, especially since the supplier saved back-end invoicing costs, and these savings theoretically could be shared with the purchaser's firm. However, in most firms, the major drawback was its acceptance by the accounting department's auditors, who operate under the premise that all goods and services must be delivered and/or performed prior to payment. In the auditor's opinion the purchase-order draft violated this basic business control principle, even though it proved a more efficient and effective tool that reduced transaction costs, gave users better service, and reduced the cost of doing business for suppliers.

One of the first and most popular low dollar-order programs was termed the "*Systems Contract.*" Systems Contracts were intended to cut the cost of requisitioning by allowing users to release requirements directly from a catalog of items, which had been negotiated in advance by the purchaser and a key supplier. Under systems contracting, purchasing controlled the source and price, then gave users the freedom to order the needed items directly. This method saved both time and transaction costs.

A systems supplier was required to maintain stock of the item or provide it in a very short lead time. Invoicing was simplified via periodic billing as opposed to billing for every transaction. This system required a longer-term relationship between the buyer and seller. It went beyond simple contract buying or "blanket orders" in that both the buyer and seller attempted to take costs out of the business process by streamlining it. The process worked very well for several firms and is still being used today.

In the mid 1990s a new concept, called the *procurement card,* became a popular method to streamline the requisition process. It was similar to the systems contract in that it required purchasing to pre-qualify suppliers up front, but it offered more flexibility in that users could select from many approved suppliers, and the number and type of items purchased under these agreements were almost endless. Users were required to track and reconcile their activities and they were limited to an individual transaction total as well as a monthly maximum. The buying firm would receive a monthly bill from the credit-card company, and the supplier was paid immediately after shipment by the card company. The supplier had to bear the credit-card company's fees, but the quicker payment usually offset the fee. This concept, which many firms adopted in the mid 1990s, has been very popular. Credit-card companies saw it as a great way to increase the share of business generated from business accounts, since prior to the procurement card they were limited to individual cards that sales representatives or other personnel used for traveling expenses.

Exhibit 3-3, Typical Paper-Based Purchasing Systems

Cash on Delivery (C.O.D.)	Telephone ordering systems
Purchase-Order Draft	Systems Contract
Procurement Cards	

Electronic-Based Systems

Starting in the mid 1970s, firms attempted to transmit data electronically. Perhaps the first attempt was called the *data phone.*

The data phone was a device that could transmit pre-punched cards over the phone. The technology was very similar to a cross between a computer modem and a fax. The buyer would enter into the unit a pre-punched card that contained the item description and quantity. The seller would receive the transmission in the form of a preprinted card at his end. This system was useful for transmitting requests for items that were ordered in standard quantities and from suppliers who had the technology. Firms also used it for maintenance items that were regularly stocked.

The data phone quickly faded with the advent of the facsimile, or "*fax*" machine in the early 1980s, since faxing was much quicker and easier than using the pre-punched cards. Now firms could quickly relay requirements to suppliers without having to mail or call in all orders. The fax allowed much quicker conveyance of other information, also, such as drawing, specifications, price lists, etc., and was a welcome addition to the purchaser's drive to streamline the purchasing cycle. Two drawbacks to the fax were that it wasn't capable of maintaining historical data and the purchaser was not automatically sure that the communication got through or was received by the person for whom it was intended.

With the advent of the personal computer, some innovative organizations began to send requirements via floppy diskette. This *physical transfer* represented the most basic form of EDI. The development of networked computing led to the use of e-mail as a communication tool, and purchasers began to use it to transmit requirements. The problems with e-mail were the need to use printed catalogs and there was no data-keeping capability. These various technologies are shown below in EXHIBIT 3-4.

Exhibit 3-4, Electronic-Based Purchasing Systems

Data phones	Faxes
Physical Transfer	EDI
E-mail	E-Purchasing

Electronic Data Interchange

In the mid 1980s an extension of the fax and data phone was being touted; this new technology was called *Electronic Data Interchange* (see Chapter 2). EDI coincided with the increasing acceptance of the personal computer (PC). EDI began basically as the transfer of purchase orders and related data from the buyer's computer to the seller's computer. EDI put an end to double entry, whereby both buyer and seller had to key in data to their respective systems before transmitting it. The American National Standards Institute (ANSI), in conjunction with buyers and sellers, developed ANSI X12, which is the standard for EDI transmission. The standard is also referred to as ASC X12 (Accredited Standards Committee). ANSI X12 established standard communication formats for EDI technology and covers several documents involved in the purchasing cycle, such as purchase orders, invoices, shipping notices, freight billings, and acknowledgments. In addition to the documents listed above, EDI permits buyers and sellers to exchange a broad array of information electronically, such as: 1) forecasts of requirements; 2) supplier shipping notification; 3) overdue purchase orders; 4) requests for quotations; 5) material certifications; 5) statistical quality analysis; and 6) order changes and cancellations.

As was mentioned in Chapter 2 there are various forms of EDI. The three major alternatives are: 1) terminal to computer; 2) buyer computer to third party (Value Added Networks or VANs) to seller computer; and 3) buyer computer to seller computer. Terminal to computer was the first and most basic form of EDI and involved the seller placing a computer in the buyer's office. The major problems with this were the multiple terminals and the fact that the buyer had to download data from his system and upload it onto the seller's terminal.

Third-party networks evolved as a service that would perform the interface between the buyer's and seller's incompatible systems. This enabled the buyer to go directly from his system to a third party to contact a large base of suppliers, eliminating multiple terminals and double data entry. Third-party providers charged a fee, however, and the response was slower due to the batch-processing nature of the service. Over time VANs became more efficient and provided a secure transaction environment seamlessly and quickly.

Buyer computer to seller computer EDI represents the closest buyer-seller linkage. In this system each party establishes a mailbox where communications are sent and received. The major advantages of this type of system are security and quick response. The buyer can scan supplier inventory and check contract price and lead times. If the part number, lead time, and quantity match requirements, the order can be entered directly. The buyer can check open-order status and shipping information, and suppliers can be sent via messages on line. The greatest disadvantage is the incompatibility of the seller's and buyer's systems.

e-Purchasing and Internet-Based Technologies

With the advent and commercialization of the Internet in the mid 1990s, firms again began exploring ways to make this technology useful in the organizational buying-and-selling process. This evolution promises again to change the way buying and selling are conducted, similar to the way earlier technologies did. In this section we will explore the electronic commerce phenomenon and its impact on the purchasing function.

Since e-Purchasing in organizations involves the processing and transmission of digitized data text, it also could include sound and visual images that are transmitted over both open networks (Internet) and closed networks (extranets) that have a gateway onto an open network. This phenomenon will impact all purchasers, and making the effort to become familiar with the technology will lead to improved organizational effectiveness.

Stealing EDI's Market Share?

A logical question being asked all over corporate America is what the role of EDI will be in this new age of Internet-based buying. There are two schools of thought on this issue. First is that we will be moving away from the EDI format as was previously mentioned. There are some strong forces behind this argument as discussed below.

Various electronic systems for linking businesses have been available for years, but these usually required costly private data networks and tailor-made software. As such, these first-generation electronic communications such as EDI were available only to an elite group of big companies and their chief suppliers.

The Gartner Group predicts that more than 40 percent of business-to-business electronic commerce applications, including traditional EDI and forms-based EDI, will be replaced by extranets by 2002. According to this prediction Internet technology will rule the e-Purchasing domain. Internet technology is a set of public-domain software standards and a global web of computer networks that make it cheaper and easier to set up in-house corporate networks and establish electronic ties with suppliers of all sizes.

The result of this technology is that supplier size is not a factor when purchasing on the Internet. Corporations use Internet technology in two broad categories: electronic communications inside the company walls (*intranets*), which are intended to replace great volumes of paperwork; and electronic communication outside the company walls (*extranets*), as a means of conducting business-to-business commerce and of sharing information with suppliers and customers anywhere in the world.

"We're trying to reduce transaction costs, and the Internet is the way to do it," said Arne Breikjern, a marketing manager at Dakota Electric Supply, a 125-person concern that sells goods ranging from light switches to telephone cable. "That's as true for us in North Dakota as it is in Silicon Valley." Dakota Electric Supply's Internet site on the World Wide Web went up last October on a business-to-business commerce service run by the International Business Machines (IBM) Corporation.[2]

What is the future of EDI?

While Web-based applications show a great deal of promise for further streamlining the procurement process, market research and firsthand accounts from industry insiders indicate that, for the time being, traditional EDI systems are not going away.

A primary reason companies say they will keep their EDI systems, at least for the near term, is money. Companies using EDI have invested a tremendous amount of time and money to develop and implement these systems, says Joan-Carol Brigham, research manager for the Internet and e-Commerce Strategies program at International Data Corp. in Framingham, Mass. Companies do not want to throw away their EDI systems," says Brigham. "They're trying to find ways to extend the life of the systems." In addition, many say that the Internet, while a powerful tool, is not yet mature enough to handle major supply-chain initiatives that are currently under way.

Terri Campbell, EDI coordinator at Avex Electronics Inc., knows just how difficult the transition can be. The Huntsville, Ala., contract electronics manufacturer recently laid the groundwork for moving its EDI systems into a Web-based format, but had to scale back its efforts after hitting some setbacks, she says. "One hurdle stems from the lack of ability to standardize Internet documents, particularly from a contract equipment manufacturer point of view, where customization is still the norm", she says. Another challenge relates to integrating systems at several levels and across all processes. "The technology is great," she adds. "We've come to a stage where everyone has e-mail and every company has a Web site. Right now it's being integrated in phases, and once companies see that a piece is working well, they will move to the next phase."

The next phase is on its way, noted Scott R. Hammed, president and chief executive of Digital Market, Inc., a Sunnyvale, Calif.-based procurement tool provider. Initially, companies moved their MRO buying processes to browser-based applications. Since realizing a savings on that front, many purchasing executives are taking similar strides on more strategic purchases, he says. "Cycle-time reductions and pressure on lowering the cost of goods sold while maintaining profit margins will help drive the growth," he adds. But how long it will take high-tech companies to reach full-blown Web-based systems is unclear. It will depend on how well EDI vendors complement their products with Web-based "gateways" to better link systems, and how fast business-to-business solutions take hold, Brigham says.

Despite the challenges, Brigham and others believe that it's not so much a matter of whether companies will make the transition, but when. The fact is, Brigham says, compared with EDI, Web-enabled procurement systems are cheaper, easier to use, and more flexible.[3]

The major question, then, is what does all this Internet activity do for the status of EDI? It appears that the predictions for their demise from many experts, like the Gartner Group in 1998, have proven wrong. In fact what has happened is that traditional Value Added Network (VAN) providers have re-engineered themselves to stay competitive in the e-Purchasing arena. Proctor & Gamble and New Jersey Public Service Electric and Gas Corporation recently selected VAN and electronic gateway services, respectively, from GE Information Services. Packard Bell/NEC and The Unilink Group contracted with VAN service Harbinger to manage their electronic supply chains.

Traditionally VAN's main focus was on providing structured, secure, proprietary pathways for EDI and the translation services. Many VANs have now re-engineered themselves to be able to provide business-to-business services via the Internet. VANs have expanded their services in order to provide multiple services. Forrester Research cites two emerging applications for VANs: first, as a gateway for companies that use the Internet for EDI transport but want to avoid the costs of building complex networks; and second, offering Web-based front ends to traditional EDI systems. For example, Packard Bell's decision to outsource to Harbinger allows it to send data to its trading partners at the harbinger.net portal in any e-commerce format including ANSI X12, UN/EDIFACT, e-forms, etc. These data are then converted into the required format before being routed to the intended recipient. Transmissions can be routed via the Internet or VAN. All transactions are completed electronically, from purchasing components to receiving payment for shipments. Harbinger's staff performs the entire operation for Packard Bell.[4]

e-Purchasing Business Models

There are three major types of e-Purchasing models that purchasers will likely use. These includ *sell-side systems, buy-side systems,* and *third-party systems.*

Sell-Side Systems

Sell-side systems contain the products or services of one or more suppliers. Registration on sell-side sites is usually free and the supplier guarantees the security of the site. The advantages to using sell-side sites are easy access and an increasing number of suppliers. Sell-side systems require no investment from the buying firm offering such sites. The major drawbacks are the difficulty in tracking and controlling spending. Sell-side sites are ideal for purchasers wishing to start e-commerce with little risk. An example of such a site is www.grainger.com.

Sell-side systems represent attempts by suppliers to increase market share through electronic commerce. The corporate Web site set up by Cisco Systems, for example, enables buyers to configure their own routers; check lead times, prices, and order and shipping status; and confer with technical experts. The site generates $3 billion in sales a year--about 40 percent of the company's total. In addition, by publishing technical documents on line and giving customers access to order information, Cisco saves $270 million annually in printing expenses, order and configuration errors, and telephone-based technical support. Its on-line market may also increase customer loyalty by speeding up ordering and order-status checking.[5]

Exhibit 3-5, Advantages (+) / Disadvantages (-) of Sell-Side Systems

+ Many Suppliers	- Tracking Spending
+ No Investment Required	- Controlling Spending
+ Ease of Access	- All sites may not be secure

Buy-Side Systems

Buy-side systems are controlled by buyers and are often tied into their internal networks or extranets. A recent article by McKinsey discusses this concept. "Buyer-controlled marketplaces are set up by or for one or more buyers, with the aim of shifting power and value in the marketplace to the buyer's side. Many involve an intermediary, but some particularly strong buyers have developed marketplaces for themselves. Japan Airlines, a big purchaser of in-flight consumable items such as plastic rubbish bags and disposable cups, posts procurement notices on line in order to find the most attractive suppliers."[6]

Other buy-side systems are tied into a company extranet, which enables the secure transaction environment. Extranets help create instant electronic partnerships among buyers, suppliers, and customers anywhere the parties have access. Extranets are also being used by purchasers to gain access to supplier product catalogs, purchase-orders status, shipping records, e-mail interactions, and invoices. The extranet enables the transaction in the transaction cycle that was discussed earlier in this chapter and enables a business to conduct its transactions much more efficiently.

"Extranets open up new sales and support channels," notes Geri Spieler, a research analyst who tracks Web-based technology at the Gartner Group, a Stamford, Conn.-based research firm. "An extranet can take a community of trading partners and bond them electronically far more efficiently than traditional methods could." Gartner estimates that within five years, eighty percent of companies will use extranets, compared to thirty percent today.[7]

The concept behind the extranet is that HTML-based information and data stored in a firm's operational database can be shared by connecting two or more companies' intranets via a secure link over the Internet. Encryption, password protection, and fire walls protect the exchanges. The major advantages for purchasers using the extranet are security and access to both real-time order status and technical data from a supplier. These advantages lower costs associated with customer service for the supplier and still provide increased service to the buyer. Extranets can provide the information that buyers need, but getting it customized requires building a good relation with the supplier. The case study below illustrates how one firm is utilizing its extranet to better serve the customer.

Using An Extranet -- A Case Study

Polymerland, a Huntersville, N.C.-based, wholly owned subsidiary of General Electric (GE), is a distributor of resins, custom compounds, and colorants used in the manufacture of plastic products. Polymerland's management decided that a new way of serving its customers demanded some innovative thinking. So Polymerland's "customer registered area," the in-house name for its extranet, offers an array of sophisticated features--and one that is unexpected.

The Web site was built for Polymerland by Proxicom, which used its own e-business software and Netscape Live Wire. The extranet site is maintained by GE's corporate Web-hosting service in Princeton, NJ.

The site was launched in June 1997, following a ten-month design and development period. Since it follows the mandates of GE's internal "Six Sigma" initiative to improve the quality of products, services, and processes, the design and development phases included extensive surveying of the expectations of plastics molding companies (Polymerland's customers).

Web-site data housed in an Oracle data warehouse on a Hewlett-Packard 9000 K570 server provide customer-specific pricing based on the user's ID, inventory availability, open orders history, and invoice status.

At no charge to its authorized customers, Polymerland provides a link to a 26,000-polymer-product database maintained by the plastics industry information systems company IDES (Integrated Design Engineering Systems) of Laramie, Wyo. Without this link, customers would have to pay for access to the IDES database themselves.

Engineers can enter the attributes and properties of a desired polymer, and the IDES database will display the items that meet their specifications. Detailed information about Polymerland's 10,000 products is stored with IDES, but customers will also see products from competing suppliers. By making IDES available, the extranet not only lets customers find products and place orders, it also assures them that they are getting the best product for their application.

Mark Rohrwasser, head of Polymerland's information systems, explains the company's expectations for the extranet: "Obviously, the idea is to increase sales, but we're trying to go beyond that and provide a solid productivity tool. By building a site for one-stop solutions, we hope to enhance customer relationships." So far the 24 x 7 site is receiving 30,000 hits per week. Needless to say, Polymerland is pleased.[8]

Purchasing Buy-side Systems

Buy-side systems (extranets) developed by the buying organization require investments in software. These systems are secure (within the organization's fire wall) and allow users to buy from approved suppliers at negotiated prices. They are the equivalent of electronic blanket contracts. Advantages to using them include: 1) the ability to leverage buying volume with key suppliers; 2) quick response to user needs; 3) the ability to allow buyers to focus on professional activities; and 4) the opportunity to control and track the collection of purchase expenditures. The major drawback is the expense of implementing and maintaining the system.

Exhibit 3-6, Buy-Side/Extranet Advantages (+) and Disadvantages (-)

+ Leverage Volume Buys
+ Quick user response
+ Frees buyer time for creative/strategic activities
+ Allows for control and tracking of purchase
  expenditures
- Capital Investment Required
- Cost to maintain system

Clearly, extranets have come of age. More mature software (streamlining everything from on-line sales to creating on-line versions of product literature), better password protection, and improved fire walls are changing the dynamics of the customer-supplier relationship. Experts offer some tips when building an extranet that effectively supports e-business requirements:

Ease of administration: Use software that makes it easy to add, drop, or alter clearance levels, so access can be controlled based on hierarchical levels.

Accommodate growth: Design the extranet to accommodate growth, as well as traffic surges from business volume changes.

Develop an interface that allows seamless data exchange: extranets provide access to information from all sorts of applications, so the interface must present data consistently.

Security: All data should be encrypted with passwords, user names, and IDs. Install a fire wall between the extranet and the internal operating system.

Ensure compatibility: Everyone who puts information on the Internet should use the same tools. Use the same hardware and software for different Internet functions.

A good source of information on technology vendors is maintained by the Gartner Group. This on-line IT vendor directory contains a growing list of suppliers both alphabetically and by category, all hot-linked to the vendors' Web sites. *See www.gartnerweb.com/public/static/atxpo.*[9]

Third-Party Intermediaries/Portals

There are several types of third-party intermediaries or portals and many services that they can provide. McKinsey has done some preliminary work identifying three types of third-party intermediaries (see McKinsey, Kenneth, Berryman, et al.). We extend their work by broadening the categories to include: *1) Buyer Intermediaries and Agents, 2) Consortium Aggregators,* and *3) Neutral Marketplaces.* We know these categories will evolve along with e-Purchasing in the future.

Buyer Intermediaries and Agents

First, *Buyer Intermediaries and Agents* either deliver a secure site for e-Purchasing or provide services such as on-line bidding and real-time auctions. Third-party buyer intermediaries develop secure trading sites that allow the buying firm to interface with many suppliers. They license their technology to many buying firms and have access to several suppliers. Third-party providers reduce the direct investment the buying firm must make, allow access to multiple suppliers, and allow the buyer to focus on professional activities. Finally, control is tracked and maintained over purchasing expenditures. There are many third-party buyer intermediaries and agents in business today and they are discussed in detail in Chapter 13. Two examples of such providers include Fisher Technologies/ProcureNet and Aribar (Wiz Net (St. Petersburg, Fla.).

Third-Party Provider Capabilities

Part of Ariba Systems capabilities focus on non-production materials and MRO supplies. Ariba's backbone is its Operating Resource Management System (ORMS), which is a global business-to-business e-commerce network for operations resources. One of the advantages to Ariba's system is that it can handle protocol differences among the various electronic communication methods, which allows companies to communicate in the format that works best for them, be it EDI, Web Page, or Commerce XML. Ariba can assist current EDI users by allowing communication through their network from any VAN. MCI-Worldcom has signed up to use this service to direct company-wide spending of operations purchases through the Ariba network.[10]

Selectica, Inc., has a new version of its Web-based configuration and selling system that lets e-commerce sites help their customers spec out and purchase complex goods and services. Selectica's ACE 4.0 features a variety of user-interface and technical improvements to bring e-commerce configuration technology to an even broader range of users. "Configuration is going to become an increasingly important technology for companies selling on the Web, particularly high-cost, high-consideration goods," said Forrester Research analyst Eric Schmitt. Web-readiness is an important consideration when weighing configurers for e-commerce, Schmitt said, because the platforms have their roots as selling tools for salespeople.

Early Web-adapter e-commerce sites such as Cisco and Dell used the technology for unassisted e-selling. Selectica has landed a number of customers, including Hewlett-Packard, which uses the system to help customers buy printers and imaging products. And Fujitsu PC is letting its site visitors use ACE to spec out new PCs. Fujitsu views the system as a "non-intrusive sales assistant," said Linda Wolff, the company's director of information technology.[11]

Third-Party Bid/Auction Providers

A second variation of the *buyer agent is on-line bidding sites*. They allow very broad market access to buyers who use the competitive bid process on standardized, low-tech items, characterized by either large variety or large volume. For example, Free

Markets Online, a Pittsburgh-based company, handles electronic bidding for United Technologies, The Commonwealth of Pennsylvania, and others. The company, as an agent, helps traditional industrial firms locate a pool of competitive suppliers for semi-complex assembly parts such as plastic injection moldings and iron castings.

Bidders are not told whom they are bidding against but see the prices that are offered by competitors. An individual bidder may submit any number of bids up to the preset deadline. An example of how this bidding process is carried out is described below.

Bidding Online -- A Case Example

United Technologies (UT) Corporation is using the services of Free Markets Online, Inc., to conduct bidding for its low-tech, pre-engineered items. The bidding starts at 9:00 a.m. with 64 pre-screened suppliers entering their bids. The bidding takes place on a lot-by-lot basis from suppliers at worldwide locations. Free Markets Online structures the bidding for its clients (United Technologies, in this case) to ensure a highly competitive marketplace. First it likes to have six to eight bidders for each item. Second, no "McBids" are allowed. This is a term for a bid that is only a few dollars less than the last offer. Third, the first lots have the most competitors, in order to give the participants a feel that it will be a highly competitive endeavor. Finally, a time deadline is set after which all bids are closed; bidding continues only when a bid occurs within 60 seconds after the scheduled closing time. Bidders don't know the names of their competitors for items bid.

Free Markets Online assures its customers that all bidding will be conducted on a secure network. Ken Brittan, vice president for supply management at UT, indicates that the auction bidding system works best for low-tech, pre-engineered items. The company prefers to negotiate key components for the jet engine, such as air foils, which are highly technical parts produced by a handful of suppliers. UT also reserves the right to decline the lowest bidder's price if it decides quality or other criteria will not be met. Free Markets Online, Inc., attempts to minimize this occurrence by making sure that in its prescreening of suppliers it takes factors such as quantity delivery, etc., into account. The process has yielded results since UT's goal was to effect 15% savings ($7.3 million). At the end of the day it had realized savings of 25% or about $12 million.[12]

Reverse Auctions

Reverse auction sites allow not only buyers to place bids but sellers to unload excess inventory. This process in theory creates a much more efficient market since both buyers and sellers have access to so many more choices in meeting their needs. In partnering with Trading Dynamics, Commerce One has added both auctions and reverse-auction capabilities to its MarketSite.net procurement trading portal. Commerce One executives feel that this capability will allow purchasers to find and acquire products more dynamically. They feel that auction services allow buyers to establish true market prices for goods or services, potentially cutting costs in the process. For sellers, it offers a new channel to liquidate excess inventories. MarketSite.net auction services take advantage of Commerce One's Common Business Library (CBL) 2.0 of XML components. Schlumberger, Inc., is one of the first Commerce One customers to use the new auction capabilities.[13]

Consortium Aggregators

The second category of intermediaries is the *Consortium Aggregator*, a group of different buyers who combine their volumes to acquire common items. In effect this voluntary group acts as the third party. The goal of this approach is to combine the purchases of several companies in order to increase their collective buying power. McKinsey uses the example of General Electric Corporation and Thomas Publishing to describe how aggregators work.

"Aggregators take a different approach, combining the purchases of several companies to increase their collective buying power. Trading Process Network (TPN), a joint venture between GE Information Services and Thomas Publishing, grew out of an initiative within GE to consolidate purchases, first within a single division (GE Lighting). It was found that at GE Lighting, procurement times were cut by 50 percent and costs by 30 percent. Other results have been a reduction in order-processing time (from a week to one day for GE Lighting) and processing costs, and 10 to 15 percent lower prices. The TPN evolved from one business, then was extended across all divisions in GE. TPN is now a Web-based service linking corporate buyers and sellers. Finally, it expanded beyond GE to include other leading corporations in a buying consortium. Forrester Research estimated that from its inception in January 1997 through year end, TPN Register's purchases would reach $1 billion. The marketplace expects to handle purchases worth $15 billion by the end of 1998."[14]

General Electric also gains revenue by charging for providing TPN to other companies for conducting transactions on its Web-based service. For example, the Textron Automotive Company, which makes parts for the auto industry, plans to shop for $500 million in materials annually using General Electric's Internet mart, where various suppliers would display their products.

Neutral Marketplaces

The third category, *Neutral Marketplaces*, is one of the most prevalent in terms of number, and several of these sites are listed in the Appendix for your review. Neutral marketplaces are set up by third-party intermediaries to match many buyers to many sellers. These marketplaces are designed by a third-party firm that compiles the products from many supplier catalogs in one place.

Neutral marketplaces allow the buyer to compare several sources at one site, are secure, and, like individual sell sites, require no investment. The major disadvantage is similar to that of the sell-side site, namely, not being able to track and control spending. Examples of neutral marketplaces include: www.echemicals.com

and www.metalsite.com. Another such intermediary is Fast Parts, which operates an anonymous spot market for the trading of over-stocked electronic components. It receives notice of available stock from sellers, then matches buyers to sellers at an on-line auction.

Internet auction sites allow buyers to search and bid for components on line from the inventory of various manufacturers and distributors. These sites provide generous savings on inventoried items that manufacturers are moving. They require no investment and offer a marketplace for those manufacturers looking to move inventory. Buyers realize great savings at these sites, usually on an as-needed versus regular basis.

Portals

Portals are another term to describe many of the marketplaces which are being formed on the Internet. The two primary categories of portals are vertical and horizontal.

Vertical portals operate in specific markets such as steel, chemicals, energy etc. As a general rule these sites tend to appeal to buyers in specific industries. Examples of companies who would be considered as vertical portals are MetalSite and CheMatch. MetalSite specializes in the buying and selling metals particularly steel. Purchasers who are in the metals buying industries are the target buyers for this site. CheMatch specializes in the petrochemicals and plastics areas.

Horizontal portals focus on a broad category of products which are purchased by buyers in many industries. Some of the more popular areas for horizontal portals include maintenance repair and operating supplies (MRO), office supplies, and surplus equipment. Purchasers in the production, service, and nonprofit areas use the products offered by horizontal portals. Thus the buyer base is much broader than those in the vertical portal sector.

The purpose of these buyer-seller portal marketplaces is to improve the market efficiencies in the markets which they serve. One purchasing manager the authors recently talked with cited how using a vertical portal was generating trememdous savings for his organization.

> "Previously we would send out bids to between three to eight suppliers for most commodities we purchased. For example, we have this grinding wheel that we use in one of our processes. Every year we would send out quotes to various suppliers. We were paying approximately $10.00 per unit. After some research we decided to use a vertical portal which handled metals and supplies. Our criteria was that the suppliers must be QS 9000 certified and have sales of at least $5million with at least 7 years of business experience. The result of the marketplace search was that we were able to locate a company in our region who gave us a price of approximately $5 per unit. The experience has been excellent to date with this supplier and our management is pleased with the savings."

As with any marketplace there are certain key issues that characterize successful portals. First, there must be a critical mass of buyers and sellers. Buyers must be able to locate suppliers that they have experience with or meet the established criteria. Conversely sellers must feel that the portal provides them with adequate quotation and business opportunities. Secondly, the site must provide content that is useful to the buyer. Prices, lead-times, and inventories should be easily accessed and be current. Many sites now provide other features such as advice on purchasing issues and articles that pertain to recent activity in the particular marketplace. Thirdly, the site must be sevure so that both buyers and sellers feel comfortable placing their transaction on the site.

Recently industry specific portals have started to form in various industries. Two of the most notable are the food and auto industry. Heinz, Kraft Foods, Proctor & Gamble and many others have agreed to develop a site that will enable these firms to purchase their goods. Meanwhile in the auto industry Ford, General

Motors and Daimler Chrysler have agreed to create a single automotive parts exchange where the billions of dollars spent by these large multinational firms would be ordered.

Why Purchasers Need to Use e-Commerce

The major advantages that buyers say they realize from conducting business via the Internet in an electronic format are are:

- Ability to find new sources
- Lower transaction costs
- Shorter cycle times
- Price reductions
- More time for value-added activitie and sourcing strategies

The major perceived drawbacks are security, training required, and time invested in locating Web sites and developing software.

Standardization Initiatives

Much like EDI in its early years, there are no standards for e-purchasing, but they are being developed and are evolving and will be implemented in a few years. Thus a key challenge for e-Purchasing today is the lack of a standard interchange format. At the moment there is a range of competing protocols used to structure and communicate catalog information. Several organizations are trying to "own the standard." Some vendors are trying to establish their standard by linking directly with a critical mass of large corporate customers. Others are creating consortiums to develop Web-based standards for purchasing MRO (maintenance, repair, and operations) end-items from inter-company catalogs, thus forcing e-purchasing software buyers to conform to the cataloger's format.

Another problem with e-Purchasing is an inability to recognize like products. For example, an e-catalog will have difficulty comparing two flashlights unless they are described identically, word for word and letter for letter. Another content-management issue lies in the maintenance of the electronic catalogs. Who will bear the brunt of the thousands of price and description changes needed to maintain the catalog--you or your vendor?[15]

There are several initiatives underway to provide a more secure and standardized system of transactions on the Internet. These include:

Setting secure electronic transmission -- a standard to ensure secure credit-card transactions on the Internet. This initiative by Netscape, Microsoft, IBM, Visa, and MasterCard makes the transaction so secure it is hidden even from the merchant.

OBI (Open Buying on the Internet) -- development of industry standards for organizational purchasing over the Internet.

Public and private key encryption -- encryption is a procedure that encodes messages in secret form. The message has to be decoded (decrypted), then interpreted. One of the most basic forms of encryption is a password. There are two types of encryption, symmetric and public key. The key is a code such as a password. Passwords are a type of single-key encryption since the key is known by both the sender and receiver. Since passwords are vulnerable, public-key encryption is used to overcome this. Users are given both a public key and a private key. What the public key encrypts, only the private can decrypt and vice versa. Thus when a buyer needs to make a secure transaction such as typing in a credit card number, the server hosting the selling site can create a public and private key pair. The server sends the public key to the buyer's browser to encrypt the information that has been typed. Only the server can decrypt the message, since only the server has access to the private key that it creates.

Authentication involves the ability to demonstrate that you are who you say you are. Authentication involves the use of a public and private key pair; it ensures that the message is going to the intended receiver. At the end of your message you use your private key to encrypt something such as your name. This encrypted information is then verified on the receiving end, since the public key will open the data and verify that the sender was you.[16]

Internet Markets Yield Lower Prices

Few studies have tested why prices are lower in Internet markets. One limited study by Strader (1999) dealing with the sports-trading-card industry found that product prices are positively correlated with search costs. Searches on the Internet result in lowest marginal search costs compared to searches in specialty card shops and at card shows. The implication for buyers is that 1) reduced search cost will result in lower prices and 2) doing business electronically needs to be supported in an environment where buyers and sellers trust each other. A trusting relationship is necessary since all sellers have more opportunity to engage in opportunistic behavior over the Internet, particularly on one-time transactions.

The Role of Relationships

Purchasing has always built on strong relationships with some of its most important suppliers. e-Business will redefine the role of communications, and yet this interaction of the buyer and seller, which is as old as civilization, will not disappear and may even increase. The Internet's size defines the potential scale of the opportunity, but not the nature of the opportunity. No one knows where the Internet is taking business, but we do know that the fundamental opportunity provided by the Internet is the elimination of limitations on electronic relations. A constraint on the Internet is that it exists in a trust economy. The Internet protocol (IP) enables any type of system to link to any other system. That opens up the three dimensions of business relationships: transaction, information, and interaction. The transaction relationship enables the routine buying of goods and services. The information relationship ranges from static displays to highly dynamic simulation. The interaction relationship ranges from passive communication via one-way electronic mail to active two-way flows and collaboration.

It's a combination of transaction, information, and interaction that seems to support Amazon.com's sustained growth. Trust is what the question of Internet security is really about: trust in contracting, payments, privacy, and safety.[17]

Intelligent Software Agents Help Buyers

e-Purchasing may increase the use of a branch of artificial intelligence known as intelligent software agents (ISAs). ISAs, a fast-growing area in information technology, can be thought of as self-contained programs with decision-making abilities that act in pursuit of one or more objectives based on their perception of the environment. ISAs complete their work autonomously in an environment that dynamically affects their problem-solving behaviors and strategies. They are being used for applications as diverse as personalized information management, electronic commerce, computer games, and management of complex commercial and industrial processes.

Three distinct classes of agents can be identified. At the simplest level, there are the *gopher agents*, which execute straightforward tasks based on predetermined rules and assumptions (e.g., which items and how many do I need to reorder?). The next level consists of *service-performing agents* that execute well-defined tasks at the request of the user (find me the cheapest airfare from point A to point B). In the last and most sophisticated category, *predictive agents* volunteer information or services to a user without being explicitly directed, whenever it is deemed appropriate (e.g., an agent may monitor newsgroups on the Internet and return discussions that it believes would be of interest to the user). These higher-level agents are expected to perform other functions such as mobility, rationality, and adaptation. Such characteristics enable an ISA to better represent its creator in the volatile WWW environment in which it operates.[18]

The attractiveness of deploying ISAs is further justified by the fact that this technology employs a new programming paradigm that has significant ramifications on transmission speeds over the Internet. Since ISAs are less bandwidth-intensive, a shortage of bandwidth caused by the sheer volume of traffic on the Internet makes for less congestion if one deploys ISAs.

Over the past few years, many ISAs have been created for different applications. These can generally be grouped into five categories:

Watcher Agents, which look for specific information (e.g., Fishwrap, JobCenter, Personal Journal)

Learning Agents, which can "tailor to an individual's preferences by learning from the user's past behavior" (e.g., Firefly, WebHunter)

Shopping Agents, which compare "the best for an item" (e.g., Bargain Finder)

Information Retrieval Agents, which help the user to "search for information in an intelligent fashion" (e.g., AppleSearch)

Helper Agents, which "perform tasks autonomously without human interaction (for network management)"

As mentioned previously (Chapter 2), e-Purchasing makes use of two entities, the client and the host server. The client server is the computer where the user creates and launches the client agent, which then travels on its own accord to a supplier's server (host server). Once the client agent arrives at a host server, the latter activates a host agent, and the transactions between the two agents commence. The client agent passes the purchasing specifications to the host agent, which then searches through the product database of the host supplier. The host agent can choose either to accept or reject the client agent's inquiry. If it chooses to accept, the host agent will go one step further to make its best offer. On the other hand, if the host agent decides to ignore the request, the client agent will be notified accordingly. In either case, the transaction is completed and the client agent proceeds to the next host server. After the client agent reaches the last host server on its list, it returns to the client server.[19]

Questions to Ask Yourself Before Starting e-Purchasing

Craig DeLano and Rex Tibbens of Mercer Management Consulting feel that four critical questions must be addressed before entering the e-Purchasing world:

1. *Do you and your suppliers have robust purchasing organizations?*

e-Purchasing will be effective only if both the buyer and supplier have robust and relatively compatible purchasing business models in place. This means well-designed policies and processes, professional staff, effective performance measures, tight controls, and appropriate organizational structures. Without these in place, e-purchasing will be harder to implement and is unlikely to be effective. Tough questions have to be asked concerning your own operations and those of current and potential suppliers:

    a. Will our organizational culture support e-Purchasing?
    b. Will our suppliers have the capabilities to handle new information-processing requirements?
    c. Are we prepared to communicate directly with each other's systems?

These first four questions may show that changes need to be made in both processes, organizational alignment, supplier relationships, and capabilities before e-purchasing can be introduced.

2.*Will your suppliers conform to your interchange format?*

Remember that there is currently no one standard interchange format. There is a range of competing protocols used to structure and communicate catalog information." Some vendors are trying to establish their standard by linking directly with a critical mass of large corporate customers. Others are creating consortiums to develop Web-based standards for purchasing MRO (maintenance, repair, and operations) end-items from inter-company catalogs, thus forcing e-purchasing software buyers to conform to the cataloger's format.

The issue for a company implementing e-Purchasing is whether its suppliers will adopt the same format. To some extent it is a question of economic clout. A large buyer typically has stronger leverage over suppliers. Understanding your suppliers' economics and where you fit in will help you estimate your leverage. However, scale alone is not always enough. The Big Three auto makers are classic examples of large companies that have not been able to capitalize on their scale. For example, they have had difficulty getting all their tier-one suppliers to conform to the same CAD/CAM system. Your "e-catalog" will contain thousands of end-items from several different vendors. Make sure you can interact easily with your suppliers, starting with the most important ones.

3. *Which software vendor should you use?*

Today, many companies provide e-Purchasing software and installation. Recently, however, the market has seen large and capital-rich ERP-software providers, such as SAP, entering the competitive landscape. This may trigger the start of significant takeovers and consolidations, although the position is not yet clear. Against this background, choosing a software vendor is a challenge.

To help your company with this challenge, it is important to treat the purchase of packaged software as a strategic sourcing decision, rather than a tactical purchase. This means focusing on the vendor rather than solely on the product. e-Purchasing software vendors will keep each other competitive on functions and features of software, so the real determining factors are vendor stability and research-and-development capabilities. Understanding which vendor will provide the most software leverage for your money becomes the acid test of the selection process. This means carefully researching and interviewing each candidate. What proportion of their revenues do they put back into development? Are they retaining good people? What is their strategy for each industry? Only by addressing these types of questions will you be able to evaluate vendors and find the best fit for your needs.

4. *How will you manage content?*

One of the greatest obstacles facing successful implementation of e-commerce purchasing systems is how to manage the data that reference and describe each product and part. e-Purchasing vendors have focused most of their attention on perfecting transaction efficiency, but have neglected to simplify the content-management process.

One problem is an inability to recognize like products. For example, an on-line catalog will have difficulty comparing two products unless they are described exactly identically. Another content-management issue relates to maintenance of electronic catalogs. Someone will have to make the thousands of price and description changes needed to maintain the catalog.[19]

References

[1]Steve Lohr, "Business to Business on the Internet: Companies Go On Line to Trim Costs and Find Ways to Make Money, Too," The New York Times. April 28, 1997, pp. 1, 9.

[2]Lohr, New York Times.

[3]Jennifer L. Balijko, Electronic Buyer News, April 19, 1999, Issue 1156, Section: Supply-Chain Management.

[4]Doris Kilbane, "VAN's Still Integral to E-commerce Picture," Automatic ID News, September 1999, pp. 26-28.

[5]Lohr, New York Times.

[6]Kenneth Berryman, Lorraine Harrington, Dennis Layton-Rodin, And Vincent Rerolle, "Current Research: Electronic commerce: Three emerging strategies," The McKinsey Quarterly, 1998, Number 1, pp. 152-159.

[7]Barryman et al., McKinsey Quarterly.

[8]Samuel Greengard, Beyond Computing, June, 1998, Vol. 7, Number 5.

[9]Gartner Group Website-www.gartnerweb.com/public/static/atxpo

[10]Ariba Website

[11]Richard Karpinski, "Selectica Updates Its System For Complex Buying," http://www.internetwk.com/story/INW19990910S0008.

[12]The Wall Street Journal, March 12, 1999. Aeppel, Timothy "Management: Bidding for E-Nuts and Bolts on the Net", p.1.

[13]Richard Karpinski, "Commerce One Readies Procurement Auctions," http://www.internetwk.com/story/INW19990909S0008. Samuel Greengard, "Extranets: The e-business Link," Beyond Computing, June 1998, Volume 7, Number 5.

[14]Barryman et al, McKinsey.

[15]Samuel Greengard, Beyond Computing, June, 1998, Vol. 7, Number 5.

[16]Charles Hofacher, *Internet Marketing*, Digital Springs Publishing, Digital Springs, Texas, 1999, pp. 105-107.

[17]Peter G.W. Keen, "Future of the Internet Relies on Trust,"

Computerworld, February 17, 1997.
[18]Li-Pheng Khoo, Shu Beng Tor, and Stephen S.G. Lee, "The Potential of Intelligent Software Agents in the World Wide Web in Automating Part Procurement," International Journal of Purchasing and Materials Management, Winter 1998, pp. 46-52.
[19]Li-Pheng Khoo, Shu Beng Tor, and Stephen S.G. Lee, International Journal of Purchasing and Materials Management.
[20]Craig DeLano and Rex Tibbens, "Is an E-Purchasing Solution Right for You?" Mercer Management Consulting, June 01, 1999.

4
Understanding
e-Purchasing *plus*

There is no doubt that the Internet is transforming business, and the purchasing function is right in the middle of the transformation. All across the U.S. and abroad chief purchasing executives are factoring e-Purchasing *plus* into their corporate visions. This focus on technology changes has electrified the function and is changing everything about how a purchasing organization operates. e-Purchasing *plus* isn't about reinventing your purchasing department. It's about streamlining your current purchasing processes to improve operating efficiencies, which in turn will strengthen the relationship you have with your suppliers.

In many organizations the value of the Web in the purchasing process is not well understood. Nevertheless, even at this early stage, the implementation of e-Purchasing *plus* is not only new but already yielding favorable results. In an October 1998 report on electronic purchasing, AMR research reported that the cost of processing an existing purchase order (PO) can be up to $175--often greater than the value of the items on the PO. Early feedback from e-Purchasing *plus* projects indicates that the cost can be reduced to $10 to $15 per order. (See Chapters 1 & 3).

What is e-Purchasing *plus*?

In Chapter 1 we defined e-Purchasing as the actions taken by the purchasing organization to integrate Internet based technologies into the role of managing the upstream portion of the supply chain to reduce costs, time and increase productivity. e-Purchasing *plus* extends this concept and is defined as "Technology used to get information to the decision makers faster." These decisions makers encompass all participants in the supply chain, such as suppliers' customers. As is shown in Exhibit 4-1, e-Purchasing *plus* extends the information capability from inside the organization to the outside organization and to all members of the supply chain to form a virtual corporation. In this new business model decision makers have access to unlimited amounts of information. (Exhibit 4-1)

What is e - Purchasing *plus*?

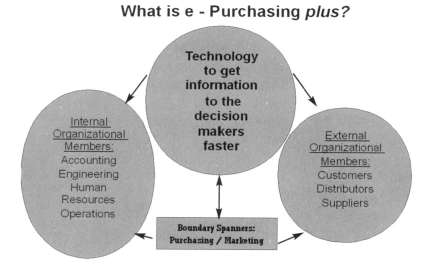

Exhibit 4-1

Imagine the information that can be made available to buyers using this on-line approach versus the conventional information process used in buying.[1] The promise of increased efficiency is why many firms' initial reaction is to focus exclusively on the Internet. Although a major part of e-Purchasing *plus* is the Internet, the transition to e-Purchasing *plus* cannot just include "using the Internet," but must incorporate a total change of process for the organization. The transformation requires the use of at least the following sets of tools:

1. Enterprise Resource Planning (ERP) -- the combining of the technologies from computers with the massively complex programs from ERP software companies, such as SAP, Baan, and Oracle
2. The Internet itself

What information do decision-makers want? The answer is understood by advertisers. With TV commercials, advertisers "pushed" information to decision-makers. The invention of the remote-control device allowed decision-makers to stop this process quickly. With the Internet, decision-makers proactively gather information; they decide what information they want and go after it. The information decision-makers want is often different from what was pushed at them by sales personnel, advertisers, etc. Let's use an example of an individual who needs information to build a wooden deck. Under the traditional system, the buyer would attempt to locate various deck plans by looking through magazines and pamphlets from the lumber store, and even perhaps going to the library. Once he finds a deck he likes he would send away for plans or calculate the material needed based on the article. In many cases time would be required to fit the plan to the individual's own situation. This retrofit would probably require several trips to the local building-supply store or lumber yard. The time and effort needed to get all the preliminary work--just to the point where the first nail can be driven--is significant.

Under the new system, the decision-maker goes on line and has the ability to review a dozen plans, select one he likes, have it instantly adjusted to fit the dimensions of his house, compile a complete parts list, order the parts, and have them delivered to his home with a step-by-step instruction sheet. The new system has compressed time and greatly reduced the cost of the search process.

Business Model

The Internet provides the ability to communicate instantly with every supplier, partner, and customer--and, in many cases, lets them communicate with each other. Partners are able to tap directly into ordering systems for earlier visibility on shipping schedules.[1]

To adjust to this new environment, companies are changing constantly. Online businesses old and new are re-creating themselves and jolting their rivals. In a desperate search for profits, they are continually redesigning their business models. Amazon.com Inc. goes from an online bookseller to selling all kinds of merchandise. Yahoo Inc. goes from a search engine to a portal. SpringStreet, a West Coast startup, goes from listing rental apartments to quoting deals on furniture, insurance, and loans, and collecting fees from Visa International.[1] [4]

A lot of the ideas will be duds, but amid the dozens of wacky proposals, propositions, business makeovers, and other e-Business madness, ideas are taking shape that will define commerce for decades to come.[4] Some of the new schemes are far from proven. Three-year-old Buy.com, for instance, sells products from computers to books at impossibly low prices to attract an audience. The company raked in $125 million in revenues in its first year of operations in 1998, and it expects to do as much as $100 million in sales this quarter. Still, it remains unprofitable and is betting it can earn most of its net on ads. Crazy or insanely smart? Only time will tell. But one thing is certain, these wild and varying approaches will rewrite the old business rules. Says John Hummer, co-founding partner of Hummer Winblad Venture Partners in San Francisco: "Whether Buy.com is successful is beside the point. They don't have to be successful to have a huge impact on all of business." So toss out that dusty old business plan, think weird, and try the unexpected.[4]

Business Model Dilemma

Harvard Business School associate professor Clayton M. Christensen believes that the Net offers a superior business model with the potential that will displace those companies unable to adapt. However, he sees a dilemma for managers who make these decisions. They must keep their present businesses healthy which may make it impossible for them to do the right thing for their future. What's best to keep the present business healthy and stock price high could ruin the long term by preventing managers from addressing the Internet.

According to Christensen, Charles Schwab is the most successful company to adopt to the new business models. Schwab is finding that its not only much less costly to do trading over the Internet, it's also more profitable to do it that way than the traditional means of addressing customers by phone or mail. Dell Computer didn't have to break their direct-sales business model to succeed with the Internet because their existing models was tied closely to the Internet. Meanwhile, Compaq Computer is trying to adopt Dell's model, but this is destructive to Compaq's current model. If Compaq can come up with a way to keep the two business models separate, they have a chance of succeeding at both. Digital Equipment is an example of a company that failed to respond to a major technology shift. It saw the personal computer coming, and it tried to attack the opportunity with its existing business model. But the PC was too small a business back then, and margins on it were too small for it to successfully compete for resources within the company. The mistake was that Digital didn't set up a different company to attack the PC. In the end, it compromised its mainstream business model, and it lost.[2]

Today there are a bewildering number of signposts, each pointing to a different business model or revenue opportunity: ads, subscriptions, transaction fees, direct sales to consumers or businesses, and commissions for matching buyers to sellers. To make the most of any of these, you must pinpoint your core strength, then turn on the creative juices to come up with new revenue streams. Figuring out a company's chief strength may be the most wrenching part of dreaming up such novel approaches.[4]

PartMiner, Inc.'s business-to-business e-Commerce model, Free Trade Zone, was developed by listening to what people in the electronics industry said they want and don't want.

1. engineers and buyers want the use of good online tools that save time in sourcing
2. engineers and buyers do not want to be charged transaction fees.
3. suppliers do not want a model that hides their brand and charges transaction fees.
4. customers and suppliers want is the ability to keep their existing relationships

The problem in existing business-to-business e-Commerce models is they insert themselves between the buyer and seller without adding value and charge a fee for it. The Free Trade ZoneTM model consists of a powerful business-to-business agent based web browser and universal trading hub with robust e-Purchasing functionality. PartMiner streamlines the purchasing process by helping customers source components from their selected suppliers all within one search. When preferred suppliers can't fill specific buyer orders, PartMiner then utilizes its intelligent infomediation to automatically become a supplier for the parts shortage. PartMiner makes its money as a supplier without stealing a customer or transaction from a preferred supplier or disrupting the existing value chain.

The Free Trade ZoneTM provides engineers and buyers with the power and speed of the Internet to source components from suppliers. It also allows suppliers the ability to reach a much larger worldwide customer base. It does this without threatening existing relationships between buyer and supplier, but adds value to the relationship.[5]

Companies have no time to do everything themselves--nor any need to. The instant communications power of the Net shatters the physical-world need to do product development, manufacturing, distribution, marketing, and customer management all in-house. Now, there are lots of specialists that can do everything from hosting Web sites to running warehouses. Look at personal-computer maker Monorail. Using intimate communications links, it has been able to out source manufacturing and assembly, financing, and shipping to other companies. The result: The company can offer among the lowest-priced PCs--and increase sales with almost no constraints.[3]

Enterprise Resource Planning (ERP)

According to www.dictionary.com-, ERP (Enterprise Resource Planning) is an integrated information system that serves all departments within an enterprise.[7]   The evolution of ERP can be traced to the manufacturing firm's use of Material Requirements Planning Systems. (See Chapter 2.) ERP systems rely on the use of packaged software rather than proprietary software written by or for one customer. Thus various ERP modules may be able to interface with an organization's own software with varying degrees of modification, and, depending on the supplier, ERP software may be alterable through programming changes to fit an existing system. A typical ERP system would include software for manufacturing, order entry, accounts receivable and payable, general ledger, purchasing, warehousing, transportation, and human resources.

During the Total Quality Management (TQM) era, the concept of "imagineering" became popular. The thrust of imagineering was to imagine what is possible and then develop the activities to make this a reality. It requires that traditional thinking come "out of the box." Imagine that a CEO arrives at his office, turns on his computer, and with the touch of a button can see how each of the worldwide operations in the company performed yesterday, the day before, etc.

Imagine that the chief procurement officer, with the touch of a button, could find out how all the purchasing organizations in the company throughout the world performed in key areas such as supplier quality, delivery, and cost savings. The technology that the ERP systems provide has the potential to allow management to reach such goals. Despite all the controversy over cost, time to implement, etc., without the technology provided by these ERP systems the dream of this type of information could not come true.

VF Corporation's External Enterprise Vision

The following case example of VF Corporation provides a glimpse into the future. VF Corporation is a $5.5 billion manufacturer of jeans and lingerie. It has brands such as Lee, Wrangler, and Rustler Jeans. It has taken them four years and spent over $70 million in software costs alone to move toward ERP. Progress has been slow, and as of November 1998 they anticipated it would take two years before the ERP software was running adequately.

Exhibit 4-2 illustrates the various systems used by VF that are required to integrate the organization's supply chain from customer to supplier. While ERP was the central focus of the system,

Company	Function
ERP	Software for order and materials management
SAP	Supply Chain functionality
i2 Technologies	Demand forecasting program
Logility	Data mining
SAS	Query tools
Brio	Apparel design package
Gerber	Demographic data
Spectra	In-store display systems
MarketMAX	Warehouse control custom-built

Exhibit 4-2 - VF e-Purchasing *plus* tools.

other modules from warehouse control to demand forecasting to apparel design have been included to provide the necessary extensions across the supply chain.

VF believes it will be a couple of years before its $100-million-plus investment pays off. Management believes that in the first year they will know by intuition how they are doing; in the second year they will build on the first year, and if they are successful, no competitor will be close to them in integrating operational data across the entire organization.

Who Is Using ERP?

A report from market-research firm Computer Economics, Inc., indicates that 18.9% of the 510 organizations they surveyed across all industry sectors have already put ERP software in place. Another 34.1% are either researching, piloting, or implementing ERP software. In the discrete- and process-manufacturing sectors, where ERP solutions evolved from material-requirements planning (MRP) systems, 35.3% of the respondents said they were researching ERP alternatives, and 40.5% said they currently have an ERP system. Distributors, which encompass all product areas and are closely linked to manufacturers, noted that 31.7% were looking into an ERP roll-out, and 18.4% said their companies have already implemented that type of system, according to Michael Erbschloe, vice president of research at the Carlsbad, Calif.-based firm.

The California company found that the ERP user community consisted of the following U.S. based companies:

- 6 of the <u>largest 10</u> companies

- 7 of the 10 <u>most profitable</u> companies

- 9 of the 10 companies with <u>highest market share</u>

- 7 of the top 10 <u>computer</u> companies

- 7 of the top 10 <u>petroleum</u> companies

- 6 of the top 10 <u>electronics</u> companies

- 8 of the top 10 <u>chemical</u> companies

- 8 of the top 10 <u>food</u> companies

The ERP Suppliers

The Gartner Group indicates that the ERP software market is dominated by large, global software vendors like SAP, Baan, Oracle, PeopleSoft, J.D. Edwards, and SSA. There are also several smaller but emerging software vendors including QAD, Intentia, JBA, Symix, and SCT. According to Advanced Manufacturing Research (AMR). Data from December, 1998 indicated five industry leaders accounted for 63% of the enterprise applications worldwide. Germany's SAP AG is the dominant supplier with 30% of the market using its R/3 software. Oracle is next with 10%, followed closely by J.D.Edwards at 9%. Peoplesoft comes in at 7%, with Baan and Putten at a combined 6%. Peoplesoft competes with J.D. Edwards for midsize companies, while Baan goes head-to-head with both SAP and Oracle for large corporate accounts.[8]

In addition to the software vendors, the global competitors in the ERP marketplace include consulting firms such as Andersen Consulting, Price Waterhouse/Coopers, and Deloitte & Touche, and systems integrators, such as CSC, EDS, and IBM.

According to Gartner, by 2000 IBM expects to be the largest

ERP services provider with greater than 10% market share world-wide. IBM's ERP primary competitors are Andersen Consulting, Price Waterhouse/ Coopers, Deloitte & Touche, Ernst & Young, KPMG, Hewlett Packard, CSC, Cap Gemini, and various niche boutique consulting firms such as Plaut and Origin.

ERP Suppliers Broaden Product Offering

After years of double- and even triple-figure growth, the enterprise resource planning market is in the middle of a painful slowdown. Companies such as Baan, Oracle, PeopleSoft, and SAP are experiencing faltering sales. Although the ERP vendors have made a valiant push into new markets such as supply chain and customer management, they have continually been upstaged in these markets by smaller, more specialized suppliers such as i2 Technologies and Siebel Systems.[9] ERP vendors are not giving in but are trying to reinvent themselves as cutting-edge electronic-business vendors -- and they're using the newly popular concept of portals to do it. Portals are Web "supersites" that provide a variety of services including Web searching, news, white and yellow pages directories, free e-mail, discussion, etc. The goal of all these products is to provide users with a personalized, browser-based entry point to everything they need to do their jobs, from accessing enterprise applications to filing expense reports and checking data on the competition. SAP combines data from its R/3 applications with other sources, creating a central site for business information intended to be used by all of a company's employees. The Web site mySAP.com- is meant to serve as a meeting place and business center for the thousands of companies that use SAP software.

PeopleSoft is working on its own portal product, the PeopleSoft Business Network. It lets customers tie all their applications to an Internet enterprise backbone and build on-line communities centering on specific business processes and information.

Oracle's portal will allow users to analyze suppliers, approve expense reports, check the status of product lines, and more -- all from a desktop with a browser. J.D. Edwards' portal is ActivEr.[10]

Renting ERP Systems

SAP, PeopleSoft, Oracle, and J.D. Edwards have entered the ERP-application rental market, which has allowed any size company to have a top-notch ERP system even if they don't have the IT resources or capital traditionally needed. All the hardware and software are maintained at the vendor's site and customers access the system via the Internet or another connection. The new SAP/EDS offering, known as EDS KeySource, costs only several hundred dollars per user per month. It includes the R/3 software license, maintenance, and network connection. The pricing is offered over a three-year period. Although the target market includes companies with an annual revenue of less than $200 million, larger companies are looking very seriously at this strategy.[11]

The Internet

The Web site www.dictionary.com- defines the Internet as follows: "The Internet is made up of more than 100,000 interconnected networks in over 100 countries, comprised of commercial, academic, and government networks. As previously discussed in Chapter 2, the Internet was originally developed for the military. It then evolved into a tool widely used for academic and commercial research. Users had access to unpublished data and journals on a huge variety of subjects. Today, the Internet has become commercialized into a worldwide information highway, providing information on every subject known to humankind."

The Internet's surge in growth has been twofold. As the major on-line services (America Online, CompuServe, etc.) connected to the Internet for e-mail exchange, the Internet began to function as a central hub for e-mail outside of the Internet community. A member of one on-line service could send mail to a member of another using the Internet as a gateway. The Internet glued the world together for electronic mail.

Second, World Wide Web servers on the Internet link documents around the world, providing an information exchange of unprecedented proportion that is growing exponentially. With the advent of graphics-based Web browsers such as Mosaic and Netscape, this wealth of information became easily available to users with PCs and Macs rather than only scientists and "computer techies" at UNIX workstations.

There has been more activity, excitement, and hype over the Internet than any other computer or communications topic since the early days of radio or television. Using the World Wide Web, thousands of companies, from conglomerates to mom-and-pop shops, are trying to figure out how to make the Internet a worldwide shopping mall. Will it become "the" model for commerce in the 21st century? Will traffic bog down like the Los Angeles freeway? Or will it become just one more option for doing business in a world rich with choices? Stay tuned![12]

Procurement looks to the Internet

As procurement organizations incorporate Internet technology into their business processes they find that it enables them to provide increased value to their organizations. The Web is becoming a growing part of the IT procurement process. Organizations are finding ways to use the Web to communicate with their suppliers. Two of the applications involve connecting with their data systems to their suppliers prior to transacting commerce.

A study in June 1998 by Purchasing magazine indicated the most popular applications.

Research potential suppliers	91%
Learn what parts a supplier makes	86%
Communicate with suppliers via E-mail	82%
Get technical data on parts and materials	80%
Gather market and economic data	76%

Keep abreast of technology trends   75%

Use on-line catalogues for contracted parts 74%

Check supplier financial records   58%

Conduct purchases on line   54% [13]

Internet Buying Standard

Standards are being developed to facilitate more buying on the Internet. A consortium called Open Buying on the Internet (OBI) has established a common architecture to guide companies and vendors in implementing Internet-based Purchasing Systems. This standard will provide buying organizations with freedom of choice and selling organizations with the ability to respond to customers' needs in a cost-effective way according to OBI.

The standard assumes that the end user is a requisitioner buying high-volume, low-dollar goods and services. In addition, trading partner relationships with 20 to 30 started trading companies were set up. The intent is to leverage the Internet, intranets, and the World Wide Web. Other considerations for the standard include real time, Internet-based ordering and approvals, user access to electronic catalogs, and order status using private catalogs. The transaction flow using the OBI standard is as follows.

1. The requisitioner views a home page of a particular firm that has a server for links to a supplier-merchant server that has an on-line catalog. The requisitioner browses the catalog and selects items.
2. When the requisitioner places the order, the supplier transmits an OBI order request to the buying organization for additional information and approval.
3. The OBI order request is mapped to the OBI order-request format. The order request is transmitted securely from the supplier to the buying organization via the Internet.

4. Administrative information is added and then the requisi-- tioner completes the order form. The order is approved and the completed order is formatted and returned securely to the supplier via the Internet.

5. Payment authorization is obtained from the payment authority and the order enters the supplier's fulfillment process and is delivered to the requisitioner.

6. The buying organization receives the billing statement and generates the payment check.

The standard was intended to have multiple benefits for both buyers and sellers. First, it should discourage software vendors from populating the Web with proprietary systems that cannot interact. Second, innovative vendors will be encouraged to jump in to ensure that their software can interact with others systems. Further information can be obtained at OBI's Web page: www.openbuy.org. [14]

References

[1]Fortune, December 7, 1998.
[2]Mike Hammer and James Champy, *Re-engineering the Corporation*, Harper Business, New York, 1993.
[3]http://www.techweb.com-/enclyclopedia
[4]Michael Hammer, *Re-engineering At Net Speed*, Information Week, April 19, 1999.
[5]Mike Hammer and James Champy, *Re-engineering the Corporation*, Harper Business, New York, 1993.
[6]Don Tapscott, *Digital Economy* , McGraw Hill, 1996.
[7]http://www.techweb.com-/encyclopedia.
[8]Industry Week, September 7, 1998.
[9]Tom Stein, "ERP's Fight For Life: The Once-Powerful Vendors Try To Adjust To A Changing, Shrinking Market," Information Week, April 12, 1999.
[10]M. Stein and Beth Davis, "Portal Push: ERP Vendors Join the Rush of Software Companies With Plans to Deliver Gateways that Integrate Applications With Other Data Sources".
[11]New Prices Make SAP's ERP Apps Affordable to Any Size Company," The Instate of Management and Administration, Managing Accounting Systems, and Technology, May 1999,
[12]http://www.techweb.com-/encyclopedia
[13]Purchasing, June 18, 1998
[14]OBI Consortium, Inc., Palo Alto, Cali

Supp
e-Purchasing p...

supply chain

Supply-Chain Management (SCM) and supply-chain systems have become one of the hottest developments in the business world during the late 1990s. Many software packages have been developed that offer enhanced analysis and scheduling algorithms that allow organizations to modify and refine their supply-chain processes.

Previous research by one of the authors has found that much confusion exists as to what supply-chain management really is. We know that managing the supply chain is a vital part of a firm's market success and profitability. A 1994 Fortune Magazine article estimated that American companies spent 10.5% of GDP just to wrap, bundle, sort, reload, and transport goods.[1] Managers who have implemented efficient systems within their operations feel there is great opportunity to reduce costs in the entire supply chain and improve customer service. What exactly is supply chain management?

The many definitions of SCM typically conclude that it:

• extends from the supplier to the final customer and

includes information flows as well as physical product flows.

• is or can be a part of an organization's strategic/competitive advantage.

• includes a group of entities/organizations that add value at each stage.

• provides benefits in terms of improved customer service with lower inventories.

• focuses on relationships as opposed to transactions.[2]

It is unclear from these definitions how SCM differs from "logistics" which in 1986 was defined by the Council of Logistics Management (CLM) as "the process of planning, implementing, and controlling the efficient, cost-effective flow and storage of raw materials, in process inventory, finished goods, and related information from point of origin to point of consumption for the purpose of conforming to customer requirements."

Clearly, The CLM definition includes materials and information flows not just within the boundaries of the firm but extending to customers and suppliers. The CLM definition also makes service to the final customer the output of the process. For most authors, it appears that SCM is nothing more than a new name for logistics. To illustrate, Dr. Roger D. Blackwell, professor of marketing at Ohio State University and author of the best-selling book From Mind to Market, says that "supply-chain management is all about having the right product in the right place, at the right price, at the right time, and in the right condition."[3]

However, managers within leading corporations Beckton Dickinson, 3M, and Xerox have a much different view of supply-chain management. It is not simply logistics extended to customers and suppliers. For these leading practitioners, supply-chain management is much more than a new word for logistics.

In this text we will use the definition used in previous

research. SCM is "the integration of business processes from end user through original suppliers that provide products, services, and information that add value for customers." The focus of this definition is on key business processes.[4]

These linkages involve changing the ways of doing business. Supply-chain terminology refers to both upstream and downstream linkages. *Upstream* are the organization's suppliers and *downstream* are the customers. Upstream in the supply chain, purchasing executives must begin to examine the structures and relationships they have in place with suppliers. Often the first action is to rationalize or reduce the supply base. The remaining suppliers may be very different from the previous ones. The automobile industry is moving toward system suppliers who provide more value-added services. For example, rather than buying components for a dashboard and assembling them in house, they now purchase the entire dashboard assembly and install it in the vehicle. Honda Motor Corporation has over 800 people in purchasing, quality control, and engineering interfacing with its suppliers as a way to strengthen the upstream supply chain[5].

Research by one of the authors recommended that firms integrate their processes by focusing on re-engineering processes and joint problem solving and using SCM as a key business strategy.[6] However, there are more than just logistics-related processes that must be integrated into the entire supply chain. Hewitt stated in 1994 that firms must use Business Process Management and Business Process Redesign as tools to maximize a firm's efficiency and effectiveness. He described the need to change information flows, practices, and authority relationships and proposed a five-stage model of logistics evolution, from stage A, fragmented technical disciplines, to stage E, integrated intra-company and inter-company supply-chain process management.[7]

Integrated Supply-Chain Model

Successful supply-chain management requires a change from

managing individual functions to integrating activities into key supply-chain processes. Traditionally both upstream and downstream
portions of the supply chain have interacted as disconnected entities
receiving sporadic flows of information over time from the organization. The purchasing department placed orders as requirements
became necessary and marketing, responding to customer demand,
interfaced with various distributors and retailers in an attempt to satisfy this demand. Orders were periodically given to suppliers, and
their suppliers, with no visibility at the point of sale/use. Satisfying
the customer often translated into demands for expedited operations
throughout the supply chain as channel members reacted to unexpected changes in demand.

Operating an integrated supply chain requires continuous
information flows, which in turn help optimize product flows. The
customer remains the primary focus of the process. However,
improved linkages with suppliers are necessary since controlling
uncertainty in customer demand, manufacturing processes, and supplier performance are critical to effective SCM. Attaining a good,
customer-focused system requires processing information both accurately and timely, for quick response systems require frequent
changes in response to customer-demanded changes.

Optimizing the SCM flow can't be accomplished without an
exhaustive review of the underlying processes. After considerable
effort, 3M managers identified seven key processes requiring analysis that support the integrated SCM approach. At some companies,
like Xerox, the return channel is also included. These key processes
are:

customer relationship management --The first step toward integrated
SCM is to identify the key customer or customer groups that the
organization targets as critical to its business mission.

customer service management -- Customer service provides the single source of customer information. It becomes the key point of
contact for administering the product/service agreement. Customer

service provides the customer with real-time information on promised shipping dates and product availability through interface with the organization's production and distribution operations.

demand management -- The demand-management process must balance the customer's requirements with the firm's supply capabilities. Part of managing demand involves attempting to determine what and when customers will purchase. A good demand-management system is continuously modeled using point-of-sale and "key" customer data to reduce uncertainty and provide efficient flows throughout the supply chain.

order fulfillment -- The key to effective SCM is meeting or exceeding customer-need dates. It is important to achieve high order-fill rates, either on a line-item or order basis. Performing the order-fulfillment process effectively requires integration of the firm's manufacturing, distribution, and transportation plans.

manufacturing flow management -- With SCM, product is pulled through the plant based on customer needs. Manufacturing processes must be flexible to respond to market changes. This requires the flexibility to perform rapid changeover to accommodate mass customization.

purchasing -- Strategic plans are developed with suppliers to support the manufacturing flow management process and development of new products. Suppliers are strategically categorized based on several dimensions such as their contribution and criticality to the organization. The purchasing function develops rapid communication mechanisms such as EDI and Internet linkages to transfer requirements quickly. These rapid communication tools provide a means to reduce time and cost spent on the transaction portion of the purchase.

product development and commercialization -- If new products are the lifeblood of a corporation, then product development is the lifeblood of a company's new products. Customers and suppliers must be integrated into the product-development process in order to reduce time to market.

return channel process - Managing the returns channel as a business process offers the same opportunity for a sustainable competitive advantage as managing the supply chain from an outbound perspective. Effective process management of the returns channel enables identification of productivity improvement opportunities and breakthrough projects.[8]

SCM and e-Purchasing *plus*

As is shown above, SCM is about optimizing business processes and business value in every corner of the extended enterprise. This enterprise extends from the supplier's supplier to the customer's customer. To be truly effective SCM needs to make use of e-business concepts and Web technologies to manage beyond the organization's internal boundaries. Reaching both upstream and downstream in the supply chain is accomplished a lot more efficiently and effectively with e-Purchasing *plus* (upstream) and other software packages (downstream).   Under these technology-enabled systems, the purchaser's firm and its suppliers can share sales forecasts, manage inventories, schedule labor, optimize deliveries, and improve productivity. The functions involved with these upstream processes included within SCM are purchasing, inventory management, and inbound transportation. Downstream involvement includes functions such as customer service, warehousing distribution, and logistics.

Traditional Supply Chain Versus e-business Supply Chain

The introduction of the Internet has changed the supply chain. The Internet provides companies that have a network of suppliers and distributors with a fast, efficient way to disseminate information and enable two-way communications. These two-way communications can be carried out over the Web using customized extranet sites, Web servers, and "groupware" (e-mail-integrated collaborative software). The following illustrates the differences between a traditional supply chain and an e-business supply chain.

Exhibit 5-1 - Traditions vs. e-Business Supply Chain

Traditional supply chain	e-business supply chain
1. Dedicated private networks	1. Shared global network
2. Networks shared as feasible within the company only with great cost/ complexity outside the company	2. Whenever demand requires with worldwide access, to whomever is authorized
3 Intra-company teams, with additional members added with difficulty and requiring customized administration	3. Intercompany teams, with global members joining and leaving quickly, securely, and with consistent, easy-to-use administration
4. Physically controlled by connection to internal corporate network and/or simple user ID and password access	4. Permission controlled, where data is accessible from anywhere on the globe, with sophisticated security for authentication and authorization
5. Physical models and face-to-face meetings with limitations such as travel and delivery of information	5. Virtual product modeling and worldwide simultaneous engineering with integrated video conferencing, Internet phone links, and visual notes[9]

Exhibit 5-1 indicates the evolutional changes that electronic supply chains will bring to organization's supply. Access to the chain is shared by all participants. Intercompany teams will be responsible to keep this information flowing. Design cycles will be completed once research is performed to determine customer needs. Real time product modeling will permit engineers within the organization to link up to suppliers' engineers. These designs will be quickly introduced into the production systems.

Reconfiguring Chrysler's Supply Chain

Chrysler Corporation was faced with a supply-chain challenge. The firm had different system configurations, legacy-style distribution methods, and security concerns. The resulting problem was that communication among its 20,000 suppliers was highly inefficient.

The company then utilized IBM's technical expertise and technological vision to assist in changing this situation. Chrysler designed an Intranet environment, which anticipates and contends with the demands of the new electronic economy. This environment, called Supplier Purchasing Interface Network (SPIN), united radically different systems so that information could be shared globally and efficiently among various Chrysler locations and with its suppliers.

The end result was that SPIN gave Chrysler and its suppliers a cost-effective and secure way of communicating and tracking auto parts, packaging, and technology. IBM's re-engineering of Chrysler's supply-chain management process means the company can now manage inventories, share sales forecasts, and optimize deliveries with great ease, and without having to micromanage suppliers and distributors.[10]

References

[1]Henkoff, R. "Delivering the Goods," Fortune, Nov. 28, 1994, pp. 64-78.

[2]Giunipero, L. and Brand, R. "Purchasers' Role in Supply Chain Management," The International Journal of Logistics Management, Vol. 7, No. 1, 1996.

[3]Dr. Roger D, Blackwell, *From Mind to Market: Reinventing the Retail Supply Chain*", Harper Business, New York, 1997.

[4]D. Lambert, L. Giunipero, and G. Ridenhower (1999), Working paper, Supply Chain Management: The Key to Achieving Business Excellence in the 21st Century.

[5]Budding, J., The Chains That Bind, NAPM Insignts, August 1993, pp. 49-51.

[6]Giunipero, L. and Brand, R. The International Journal of Logistics Management, Vol. 5, No. 2, 1994, pp. 1-9.

[7]Hewitt, F., Supply Chain Redesign, The International Journal of Logistics Management, Vol. 5, No. 2, 1994, pp. 1-9.

[8]D. Lambert, L. Giunipero & G. Ridenhower, 1999.

[9]IBM Webpage

[10]IBM Webpage

Section 2
Making e-Purchasing *plus* a Reality

6
Where to Begin?

So where does your purchasing department begin in order to make the transition to e-Purchasing *plus*? First you must identify how your purchasing organization contributes to the most critical key process in any organization, namely, managing relationships with your final customer. Processes such as supply-chain management and e-Commerce can help make positive contributions to the customer's overall satisfaction. Implementation of e-Purchasing *plus* activities represents an important part of the supply chain that impacts the final customer.

Business Objectives

Benchmarking Partners' has done and continues its ongoing research of 350 ERP implementations. The firm feels that focus and business objective of these projects often depend on the specific industry. Exhibit 13-1.

Business State	Examples	Focus/Objective
Maturing Markets/Commodity Products	Chemicals , Metals, Autos	Reduce cost of business
Rapid Growth Markets	Electronics & Telecommunications	Enhance capabilities enabled by technology

Exhibit 13-1 - Business Objectives for e-Purchasing Systems

The reader should keep in mind that these are general guidelines and each organization, regardless of its business, should make sure that its objectives for the e-Purchasing *plus* program are clearly stated throughout the entire organization.

Starting e-Purchasing *plus*

When undertaking e-Purchasing *plus* activities, the organization will undergo a major change process, regardless of which steps are undertaken first. The steps in Phase should be started as soon as possible in order to determine the ability of the organization to accept the e-Purchasing *plus* activities. As previously discussed in Chapter 6, Phase I has three steps:

1. Establishing the management environment -- Leadership, Vision, Commitment, Change process
2. Understanding purchasing's customers and their needs, both internal (CEO, CFO, etc.) and external customers (suppliers)
3. Determining the purchasing strategies

Since most purchasing organizations have some activities in place, the selection of which of the 2 steps in Phase II to focus on may vary by activity. Some areas have already been re-engineered and now need to identify tools that will help speed the implementation process. Meanwhile, other activities have had little work done over the years and may need re-engineering. The case studies provided in this book should provide some guidance based on what other companies have done.

e-Purchasing *plus* Transformation Guidelines

Making the e-Purchasing transformation is not an easy task. Here are ten overriding points you might want to consider using to help guide your program efforts:

1. *Carefully build your team*

The rapid changes in Internet technologies will require a team of both functional and Web experts who are willing to make the commitment. The team will need to devote much time and energy in order to guide the plan to its completion. Since Web-based technologies will change, they will have to devote considerable time to these issues. A plan developed by this team will need to be monitored and changed when and as needed.

2. *Scan the environment* -- Research, interview, and research

The Internet company landscape is filled with many firms offering solutions (see Chapter 13 and Appendix). Your organization needs to determine what it wants to do on the Internet. This could range from placing orders for small-dollar items there to becoming an automated, integrated enterprise. Research the third-party providers and firms you think would help you attain your goals and have your team interview the firms. Make sure to visit other companies that have adopted the technologies you are considering and carefully note if the environment is similar to the environment that you now operate in or visualize yourself operating in. Once you have narrowed the list of firms, consider the establishment of costs and a tentative time frame.

3. *Obtain Management Support*

You will need a budget, some funds, and expected savings in order to implement your plan. If you have a well-thought-out plan and have made reasonable estimates of the proposed savings and benefits, gaining the support of top management should not be all that difficult. Management is aware of the hype surrounding the Internet and they are anxious to hear your plans. In fact it is much better to have and present a plan, before top management hires a consultant to deliver one. Actually, you may want to look to a purchasing consultant for guidance on the e-Purchasing issue as a start. Don't overlook the need for people, acceptance, and training costs needed to change skill sets in the new e-Purchasing environment.

4. *Tie e-Purchasing to your broader e-business strategy*

e-Purchasing does provide efficiencies for purchasing itself by reducing transaction costs, freeing buyers to be more strategic, and adding value. Don't lose sight of the bigger picture, for another big payoff is tying e-Purchasing to ERP, the firm's Web strategy, and its interface with the organization's customers. e-Purchasing is only one part of the entire change of a firm's business model. Thus it is important to understand how your strategies fit the bigger, overall picture. Without this integrated linkage, your e-Purchasing plans could be in trouble.

5. *Perform a Supply Chain audit and/or review*

The supply chain needs a complete analysis and top-down review of the entire process. For example, orders to key suppliers may flow directly to suppliers, and the purchaser reviews the orders after the fact and monitors quantities and ship dates. The supply chain may need more integration of processes at the boundaries of the business model. One of the challenges for purchasing is reviewing the nature of relationships with all suppliers. The overall review of the supply chain starts at the front end and continues through the facility and back to the suppliers' stock-replenishment, shipment, and billing processes. It will become common practice for your firm's customers to check real-time status of their orders, through your firm's extranet, all the way back to component suppliers.

6. *Speed and Convenience are Key Requirements*

The Internet is perceived by those using it as an advancement over current technologies. Thus your e-Purchasing system must be fast and convenient for all users who have interface with it. If for some reason it is cumbersome, difficult to operate, and generally unfriendly to users, you will quickly lose support.

7. *Manage and improve supplier relations and performance*

Your suppliers need to understand how your e-Purchasing system will affect them and what costs they will incur by using it. In systems allowing direct customer linkages, they will need to understand that requirements will come from many users. It is important for you to help them modify their processes in order to improve performance and efficiency. Finally, they need to understand your processes and how they fit into your overall supply chain.

8. *Change, Change, Change*

You will always be involved in making improvements and changes to your system, since the only constant will be system change and system enhancements. For example, is Web-based buying going to change the way people see their suppliers or will buyers feel free to change suppliers more frequently? Structuring and segmenting your relationships with your suppliers will become more critical. However, on non-strategic standardized items such as MRO and basic commodities, the advantage of outright bidding and buying will become much more apparent thanks to access to worldwide sourcing and the consequent savings.

9. *Maintain a strategic focus*

If the Web is to offer you significant savings you must continue to be driven by the strategy of selecting those sources that provide the best overall value. Don't fall prey to the seductiveness of short-term price savings that become long-term cost increases. Continue to evaluate suppliers based on lowest total costs. Don't overlook long-term relationship benefits and such key savings areas as inventory, service, etc., in order to realize a short-term price savings.

10. *The sales interface may change*

Over time the Internet may turn out to be more of a price leveler than a price cutter. According to economic theory, when there is perfect information in a market, prices tend to converge. The Internet is giving buyers access to worldwide pricing. This will make it more difficult for producers to use localized pricing, and even tiered pricing, in certain markets.

7

Implementing e-Purchasing *plus* Overview

There are *two phases* in the implementation of e-Purchasing *plus*; *Phase I* is the preparation of the organization and *Phase II* involves the actual implementation of the project. We will focus primarily on the implementation itself, but will examine organizational readiness in general, since it is imperative that the organization be prepared in order for the new technology to be successful.

Over the years organizations have gone through a variety of change-of-the-decade concepts such as Total Quality Management (TQM), Just in Time (JIT), benchmarking, empowerment, etc. Each of these programs has required an organizational readiness phase. The steps outlined in Phase 1 are essentially the same as those used during the Total Quality Management era of the 1980s and are discussed in more detail in one of the author's prior books, *TQM for Purchasing Management*.[1]

Organizational Readiness for e-Purchasing *plus*

Getting the organization ready for e-Purchasing *plus* (i.e., Phase I), has three steps (as mentioned in Chapter 6).

117

Step 1. Establishing the management environment--Leadership, Vision, Commitment, Change process

Step 2. Understanding purchasing's customers and their needs-- Internal (CEO, CFO, engineers, maintenance, etc.) and external customers (suppliers)

Step 3. Determining the purchasing strategies

Establishing the Management Environment-- Leadership, Vision, Commitment, Change process

The objective of this step is to have management demonstrate clearly the leadership needed in order to establish the conditions that will make the process flourish. Management's objective is to create a new, more flexible environment and culture that will encourage and accept change.

This includes gaining the support of top management. After support is secured, the leadership from key managers who understand the vision of the organization for e-Purchasing *plus* is necessary. This change process will encounter resistance and problems. Thus operating managers must be committed to seeing this vision carried out. To be successful they need solid and unwavering support from the top. One of the first steps in getting management up to speed is to familiarize them with the need to use these new technologies.

Advantages of buying on the Internet

One of the keys to establishing the environment for management support is to sell management on the tremendous benefits of making these systems work. Elizabeth J. Beard of Fisher Technology Group outlines three major advantages of buying on the Internet.

1. Buyer benefits include savings via reduced product prices

and reduced procurement-processing costs. Cost avoidance is realized by streamlining the back office, avoiding cumbersome legacy requirements, ensuring that corporate rules are followed, and improving the supplier consolidation process.

2. User satisfaction goes up by offering users ordering options, simplifying complex processes such as the MRO process by offering multiple supplier access, and reducing errors.

3. Supplier benefits include increased sales, improved market share/position, enhancing image, and direct contact with end-users. Suppliers also lower costs via processing, reduced errors, and improved operating income.[2]

Skepticism toward e-Purchasing *plus*

While there are advantages to Internet buying there will be those in your organization who aren't convinced of e-purchasing's advantages. e-Purchasing software is still immature and the benefits require the enormous task of integrating it with existing legacy systems. Dan McMenamy, controller for the Hyatt Regency Chicago, stated that on-line purchasing systems still have a long way to go before there are universal catalog formats and a rich electronic-payment infrastructure to settle deals on line.

A recent survey of purchasing agents found similar opinions. The survey, taken at the National Association of Purchasing Management's (NAPM) 1999 annual conference, found widespread unhappiness with current e-purchasing tools. Some 40 percent of the 212 respondents, users of both enterprise resource planning (ERP) and dedicated electronic purchasing systems, explained that they had to use more than one system to do basic purchasing and contracting. Another 86 percent said that they wanted a single-entry search engine for doing comparison shopping, but only 25 percent have this as of yet. One third of the purchasing managers said they could not easily place orders against a master contract, even though

94 percent said they wanted to do so.

Results of another survey, sponsored by e-purchasing-software maker American Management Systems, supported the NAPM findings. "There is tremendous dissatisfaction with the procurement systems, which have not kept up with the changes in the purchasing processes," said John Bermubez, vice president of research at AMR Research. Bermubez provided one extreme example of a large truck manufacturer that deployed Baan's ERP system but kept its 25-year-old e-purchasing/EDI system in place.[3] Thus it is important to anticipate negative comments and lack of support from certain individuals who are fearful of the changes e Purchasing *plus* will bring. Top management must constantly be made aware of the immense benefits as well as the potential pitfalls that such an undertaking will bring. Only by presenting a balanced viewpoint will the project gain the support necessary to see it through to implementation.

Understanding Purchasing's Customers and their Needs--Internal (users--e.g., engineers, maintenance, etc.) and external customers (suppliers)

The objective here is genuinely to understand purchasing customers and their requirements. For the purpose of this approach, suppliers are to be considered customers. If suppliers are provided the correct information about ordering, schedules, specifications, etc., they can better provide the product and services needed.

Internal customers such as management personnel have varying input on e-Purchasing *plus*. The key is to work in a team environment with management to establish the plan, funding levels, and goals for the project. Finally, internal customers need to be involved in order to establish the methods and process for their involvement in the purchasing cycle.

One of the first steps to be taken is to determine what buyers and purchasing managers want out of the Web. This then enables them to communicate clearly to users what e-Purchasing *plus* will offer users and help the team make modifications to meet user requirements.

What do Web Buyer's want?

1. Speed -- find it fast

2. Integration -- do not have to key in the same information twice

3. Information -- see detailed product information in order to shop, compare, and order

4. Ease of Navigation -- 3 clicks or fewer

5. Navigation options -- find an item by name or browsing

6. Contact -- telephone, e-mail or fax a human

What do Purchasing Managers Want?

1. Empower user to buy standard and low dollar items

2. Similar look among supplier websites

3. Training-free navigation -- a system that is intuitive to navigate

4. Integration with their own company's back-end systems

5. Electronic catalog customized to the buyer requirements

6. Privacy and security

7. Controls on purchase limits and access

8. Enhanced search capabilities

9. Easy access to the system for valid users and authorized suppliers [4]

These wants will go a long way in determining the format that each organization implements for its e-Purchasing *plus* technologies.

Determining the Purchasing Strategies

Purchasing strategies are successfully executed only through well-designed business processes. Information technology initiatives are successful only when they are aligned with the business processes that support the strategies. With these two things in mind, the objective is to select purchasing strategies appropriate to the needs of the customer. Rarely is the first set of selected strategies successful. This step means *kissing a lot of frogs before you find a prince*. If you stop at the first frog you will have a failed project. One of the pitfalls of e-Purchasing *plus* is that a few failures dim the organization's enthusiasm for it. Remember that the overall strategy is to strive continually for a virtual on-line environment where requisitions, orders, and information flow seamlessly from user (requisitioner) to purchaser to supplier to delivery.

Does Technology Drive the Strategy?

The Gartner Group's surveys indicate that business-to-business electronic commerce will affect more than 90 percent of procurement organizations in 1999. This electronic commerce has created a situation where technology is dictating strategies. Prior to the infusion of technology, the accepted planning process included defining the strategies and then identifying and implementing the systems that support them. In the world of the Internet, the old system is backwards. According to Ted Rybek, chairman of the Benchmarking Partners, Cambridge, Mass.[5], "The first generation of ERP systems dealt with the cost of ownership and told you what happened in your business. The new breed of decision support systems answers the question, "What should be happening?" These new systems are dictating the strategies that must be employed. For example, if your competitor is using the latest ERP system and buying on the Internet with overall lower costs than your buying organization, then you may be forced also to use a system that will allow you to buy on the Internet, even if that wasn't your strategic direction. Likewise if your suppliers or customers are using a specific technology, you may be forced to implement that technology in order to play in the game at the same level.

Previous chapters have discussed leading examples of CISCO, Dell, General Electric and IBM who are considered leaders in e-Purchasing. Several of General Electric's divisions use the Internet to request bids on parts and equipment. They also deal directly with suppliers over the Internet. GE estimates it will save $500 to $700 million off its purchasing costs over three years and cut its purchasing cycle time by 50%. GE expects that in five years it will purchase the majority of everything it buys through this Web-based bidding system.

Dell sells equipment directly to its customers, while Compaq sells through its distributors. Compaq could be at a disadvantage if its distributor costs are higher than Dell's direct-selling costs. If Compaq then sells directly it will undermine its own distribution. Companies such as Compaq and IBM will have to reevaluate how they go to market. Competitors of these two firms may find themselves using e-Purchasing plus to keep up. They will need to make sure their organizations are ready.

Is e-Purchasing *plus* the Right Strategy?

IBM thinks it is according to Chairman Lou Gertsner:"--- e-business is not a technological change. It's a fundamental change in the way business will be done in their industries -- aided, abetted, supported, and enabled by technology."

e-Purchasing *plus* is a major element of IBM's thrust and permeates many aspects of IBM. IBM's plan include accelerating e-Purchasing transformation to enhance IBM's ability to do business with current and prospective suppliers. "Our goal is to drive the rapid transition of Procurement into an IBM showcase for e-business. The Internet offers vast opportunities for cost savings, collaboration, market intelligence gathering and improved transaction processing." Gene Ritcher, VP and Chief Procurement Officer.

IBM's e-Purchasing strategy is to exploit the web in all aspects of the procurement process through global, replaceable solutions. IBM's goal is to enable 10,000 suppliers to transact via the

Web in 1999 and achieve a totally paper less trading environment in 2000.

References

[1]James Cali, *TQM for Purchasing Management*, McGraw Hill, New York, 1992.

[2]Elizabeth Beard, Fisher Technology Group Presentation, Developing Excellence in Purchasing Management Program, Florida State University.

[3] Ellis Booker, Internet Week, Issue 768 (June 7, 1999), "Enterprise Users Poke Holes In E-Procurement," Section: News & Analysis.

[4] Kathleen Melymuka,"WHAT DO WEB BUYERS WANT?", Computerworld (October 26, 1998).

[5]Fortune, December 1998.

8
Implementing e-Purchasing *plus* in Production Buying

Case Studies

A listing of some of the purchasing process activities and case studies for production procurement are summarized below (Exhibit 8-1). We will present each of the procurement processes in

Exhibit 8-1 - e-Purchasing Case Study Summary

Procurement Activity	Case Studies
Source selection	Newport News Shipbuilding
Forecasting requirements	Aspect
Negotiating	Sprint
Contracting & Ordering	Solectron
Delivering & Invoicing	Federal Reserve Papa John's International
Integrated Purchasing Systems	Oracle, NetBuy, Power Center

general terms. This is followed by a short summary case describing a portion of the process, and finishes with two integrated procurement cases. The cases are short and provide a brief look at the experiences of several organizations.

Newport News Shipbuilding -- Source Selection

Problem: Identifying the right part from hundreds of thousands of parts used in aircraft, some used since WWII. Information was stored in a variety of systems, which all had different ways of describing and sorting parts. Newport News simply had no method to view existing part information in a consolidated, easily accessible format. The company wanted to reduce inventory levels and consolidate purchases with strategic suppliers.

Solution: ERP system (SAP R/3) and Aspect Development's Component and Supplier Management products.

Results: As of this writing, information from 3.5 million components has been migrated, standardized, and consolidated to produce a coordinated system.[1] This firm is now in the process of trying to consolidate its supply base in order to obtain needed parts at lower costs.

Aspect, Inc. -- Forecasting Requirements

Problem: Determining aggregate requirements across multiple manufacturing locations.

Solution: Aspect's Strategic Sourcing Management Solution "talks" to, collects, and consolidates information about volume, pricing, inventory, supplier performance, purchasing history, and future requirements across new and legacy systems that can't talk to each other.

Results: Potential for immediate five to twenty percent discounts from suppliers thanks to improved forecasting and leveraging opportunities.[2]

Sprint -- Web Auctions/Negotiations

Problem: High costs of purchased items and a need for greater control over these expenditures.

Solution: Sprint used A.T. Kearney, a global consulting company that developed the Internet Auction, as part of its Strategic Sourcing program. The Internet Auction replaces traditional round-one negotiations with suppliers, cutting 70 percent from proposal cycle times.

With Kearney's Internet Auction, suppliers don't need special software or fee-based connections, only a Web browser and a pass-word. Any laptop connected to the Internet will link the supplier to the auction. That means participation by more qualified vendors. Internet bidding also means that buyers and suppliers aren't dependent on corporate networks, which are sometimes subject to failure. (See Chapter 3 for further discussions of Internet auctions.)

Results: The Internet-based auction for Sprint attracted 85 qualified suppliers vying for more than $75 million in telemarketing-services contracts for the global communications company. The four-hour auction streamlined the negotiation process by at least three weeks, facilitated the introduction of diversity in the supply base, and improved the average proposal prices by five percent. This real-time, on-line bidding process has worked well for Sprint. As a result of the sourcing process, Sprint expects to realize many benefits, including significant service improvement as well as cost reductions.[3]

Electronic Data Interchange

Definition: Electronic Data Interchange (EDI) is the computer-to-computer exchange of business documents in a public standard format. EDI provides for paperless transactions between and within companies. EDI is a method of ordering that became popular in the mid 1980's. Examples include transmitting data from a customer's purchase-order system directly to a supplier's order-entry system, or from a supplier's billing system directly to a customer's accounts payable system.

Some quick facts about EDI are listed below (additional discussion of EDI is provided in Chapters 2 & 3):

• The National Association of Purchasing Management (NAPM) reported in May 1998 that 67% of companies surveyed indicated that they use some form of electronic purchasing, and 75% of those using electronic purchasing said they used EDI.

• Several organizations are involved in EDI Worldwide:

• ANSI (American National Standards Institute) coordinates and approves, within the US, standards that are set voluntarily by the US industries.

• ASC X.12 (Accredited Standards Committee X.12) develops uniform standards for the electronic interchange of business transactions.

• EDIFACT (EDI For Administration Commerce & Transport) is a United Nations standards-setting organization for EDI.

• EDIFICE (EDI for Companies with Interest in Computing and Electronics) is the counterpart of EIDX for guideline development in Europe.

• EDIMAN (EDI For Manufacturing) is the counterpart to EIDX in Singapore.

• EIA (Electronic Industries Alliance) is the secretariat to EIDX and partner in promoting EDI and electronic commerce in the industry.

• EIAJ (Electronic Industries Alliance of Japan) is the counterpart to both EIA and EIDX for guideline development in Japan.

• PAEB (Pan American EDIFACT Board) is one of six regional teams participating in the EDIFACT standards development.[4]

XML -- "Web-based form of EDI"

XML, the eXtensible Markup Language, defines a universal standard for electronically exchanging data. XML was designed to enable business data to be served, received, and processed on the Web as easily as HTML (hypertext markup language). HTML is the document format used on the World Wide Web. Web pages are built with HTML tags, or codes, embedded in the text. XML provides a flexible, extensible mechanism that can handle the gamut of "digital assets," from highly structured database records to unstructured documents and everything in between.

The Worldwide Web Consortium (W3C) recommended the XML 1.0 standard in February, 1998, and it is being widely and rapidly adopted as a standard for document and data exchange in a variety of markets. XML is gaining wide industry support as well from vendors like Oracle, IBM, Sun, Microsoft, Netscape, SAP, and others. Web Methods, Inc., is considered the leading supplier provider of XML-based solutions for business-to-business e-commerce and integration, and as of this writing was teaming up with SAP for solutions regarding the enhancement of automated procurement.[5]

An example of what XML can do is as follows:
Whackmeister lawn mower company has been buying about 10,000 wing nuts per week from the same supplier for 10 years. Since bringing two more factories on line however, it has found that its regular supplier is unable to provide the additional 6,000 wing nuts it needs to fill the new capacity.

XML acts as a universal data format to describe each day's price and available inventory of wing nuts from each of Whackmeister's many suppliers. Whackmeister's purchasing manager can prototype, test, and deploy a simple application that polls multiple suppliers' XML-based Web catalogs and aggregates each of their pricing and inventory quotes automatically into a single Web page from which he can place orders directly. The orders can then be passed into Whackmeister's internal order-tracking database to fulfill each factory's needs as they arise.

The purchasing manager receives a daily report of orders for Whackmeister's lawn mowers The purchasing page lists the latest price and available units from a set of suppliers. The purchasing manager can sort this list according to his needs. For instance, if price is critical, he can sort suppliers by price so that the least expensive supplier is easiest to find.

When the choice has made, he clicks on the company name, which is a link to a purchase order (PO). This electronic purchase order is a form where all of the appropriate information that Whackmeister needs has been automatically provided. This information includes the company's supplier number, main contact person, preferred shipping methods, and price. The purchaser picks the appropriate factory from a list that fills out the shipping address on the form, and enters the volume of wing nuts he wants to buy. The form is submitted electronically, instantly translated into the supplier's automated PO format, and then put into the supplier's order system.[6]

Solectron -- Contracting and Ordering

Problem: Needed an electronic way to exchange product-design information among trading partners in Printed Circuit Board (PCB) manufacturing. Contract manufacturers like Solectron have been purchasing plants from their customers. Through these actions they are rapidly taking on a large amount of the high-volume work, for new and existing products. A large part of the cost of taking on new customers is creating custom interfaces for receiving design information and getting it into production quickly

Solution: Solectron has teamed with Agile Software and distributor Marshall Industries to form an electronic partnership. Agile is a fast-growing Product Data Management (PDM) vendor with several hundred customers in the electronics industry. Solectron and its partners developed a solution based on the eXtensible Markup

Language (XML) standard for electronically exchanging data (see Chapter 3). The standard covers the Build Package, Engineering Change Orders(ECO), deviation reports, and Bill of Material (BOM). XML is a useful vehicle because it is becoming widely supported as a tool for importing and exporting data to a variety of applications. The biggest advantage of this initiative is that the semantics for XML messages will now become the standard way of trading information.

In addition to its work on the XML standard, Agile intends to provide two Java applets (small software program enbaling users to run various applications), one to read and view the files and another to package data and check them for consistency. While Agile will provide this capability in its PDM product, a contract manufacturer will be able to redistribute these applets to its customers (OEMs) for use with other vendor's CAD, PDM, and ERP systems. Agile indicated that these applets would be distributed at no charge to help promote the standardization process.

This initiative is important because instead of just extending the customer's systems into the contract manufacturer, it allows for the contract manufacturer to receive standardized data from many different customers, regardless of which enterprise applications they use.[7]

Federal Reserve -- Invoicing Payment System

Problem: Needed common solution for Financial Electronic Data Interchange (FEDI) to all financial institutions.

Solution: Bottomline Technologies was selected by the Federal Reserve Bank to provide FEDI (Financial Electronic Data Interchange) translation software to all financial institutions. The software is both a Windows 95/NT and DOS product offering.

Products include PayBase, Bottomline's 32-bit payment technology suite, which is a complete client/server payment management and integration solution. PayBase-Payment Server32 is for the entire enterprise and PayBase-Payment Workstation32, for a single-station, provides a multi-user, multifunction system for any size organization. PayBase will interface with virtually any existing application, capture any requested information about the payment streams, and produce any type of disbursement--from paper checks to direct deposits to bank-compliant electronic payments.

When fully implemented, PayBase 32 features integrated check printing, fraud protection, and electronic payments. In addition, PayBase 32 offers a sophisticated remittance-delivery solution, which transmits the payment addenda detail either electronically or via paper. This provides organizations with the ability to pay via direct deposit and simultaneously to notify the employee or vendor via company e-mail.[8]

Papa John's International, Inc. -- Invoice Payment

Problem: Needed a consultative business partner that could offer the technical expertise and software tools necessary to support the growing payment needs.

Solution: PayBase 32 provides Papa John's with a disbursement system that manages high levels of accounts payable (A/P) and payroll output. The company utilizes Bottomline's PayBase to process weekly payroll for over 13,000 employees in over 475 corporate restaurants, as well as employee payroll for several Papa John's franchises. Overall, the operation creates 52,000 checks a month. Accounts payable payments for approximately 30 Papa John's vendors total between 800 and 6,000 checks each month.

Integrated Procurement

Definition: A system developed to include all or many of the activities in the procurement process, from intelligence gathering to contracting to paying the supplier.

Oracle Corporation -- Integrated Procurement System

Problem: Overall costs of purchases were too high.

Solution: Oracle's Strategic Procurement provides on-line access to supplier and commodity spending across a company. The system allows for the posting of RFQs for supplier review and response on the Internet, and has Web Requisitions and on-line supplier catalog access. It is workflow-enabled, has document-approval routings, and determines whether a supplier should be paid on receipt of goods or receipt of invoice.

For production procurement, Oracle Supplier Scheduling helps to integrate supply-chain partners by providing the automatic generation of planning schedules with forecast information or consolidated shipping schedules with firmed-up requirements. After being automatically generated, these schedules are sent to the supplier via EDI or simply posted on the Web for easy viewing and downloading by the supplier.

Results: The visibility of supplier and commodity spending allows the user to set up the right contracts with the right suppliers, and to monitor internal and supplier compliance. Supplier performance can be measured against targets for cost, quality, and delivery. The system enables the user to eliminate all non-value-added steps, increase procurement efficiency, and reduce administrative effort and cost.[9]

NetBuy Corporation -- Integrated Procurement System

Problem: The procurement cycle was too long.

Solution: NetBuy Corporation (Laguna Hills, California), an e-commerce purchasing service for electronic components, has a Web site (www.netbuy.com) with tools that allow users to search for multiple parts, track order-to-dock shipments, and upload bills of material. NetBuy has over 329,000 unique parts from 56 franchised distributors representing 1978 manufacturers. The system provides for multiple-part searches and the uploading of bill-of-material spreadsheets and files. It allows the user to get quotes and check availability from 50 distributors for up to 500 parts.

Results: Increases buyer's ability to access data and make purchasing decisions. By using shortcuts, users can immediately quote and purchase components from multiple distributors, a process that often takes several days through conventional practices. It gives the buyer the best selection, accommodates low-bandwidth connections, and provides dramatic shortcuts to the procurement process.[10]

Power Center -- Integrated Procurement

Problem: The data in various systems were in need of consolidation.

Solution: Informatica Power Center 1.5 is an enterprise-data-integration hub that integrates and unifies the many diverse tools--and the various user groups--that populate today's enterprises. It enables large organizations easily to transform legacy, relational, and ERP (enterprise resource planning) data into reliable information for strategic business analysis.

Within an enterprise decision support solution, PowerCenter is responsible for extracting data from operational sources, enriching it for decision support, cataloguing it for use and reuse, and delivering it to powerful business-intelligence and analytic applications. PowerCenter 1.5 is the industry's first meta data-driven product to deliver the essential requirements of an enterprise-data-integration hub, including: consolidation, cleansing, and customization of data; integration of operational and analytical resources; and centralized management of distributed resources.[11]

References

[1]Aspect Web page.

[2]Aspect Web page.

[3]A.T.Kearny Web page.

[4]Electronics Industry Data Exchange Association.

[5]Oracle.com : XML : Technical Whitepaper - An Oracle Technical Whitepaper November 9, 1998.

[6]Andy Dzamba, "Get Ready to Say Good-bye to Expensive EDI Technology", The Institute of Management and Administration, Managing Accounting Systems and Technology, September - 1999.

[7]IBM Web page.

[8]Botttomline Technologies Web page.

[9]Oracles Web page.

[10]Jennifer L. Baljko, "NetBuy enhances Website with Buyer-Friendly Tools", Electronic Buyer News, June 7, 1999, Issue 1163.

[11]Informatica Webpage.

9

Implementing e-Purchasing *plus* in Non-Production Goods and Services

Non-production goods and services are all those items organizations need in order to operate and support the operations required to produce a product or deliver a service. Typical items include maintenance, repair, and operating (MRO) supplies, office supplies, outsourcing contracts for services, etc. Many of these items, particularly MRO and office supplies, are low-dollar items that collectively represent a large number of items and have high transaction costs. These items make ideal candidates for an e-Purchasing *plus* approach.

As stated earlier in Chapter 1, buying on the Internet is increasing significantly, and, according to Forrester Research, Inc., of Cambridge, Mass., US business-to-business Internet transactions are expected to account for $327 billion in trade by 2002. Companies are buying over the Web to cut costs, speed service, push purchasing down to the employees who use the goods--such as office supplies and airline tickets--,and strengthen the connection between buyers and vendors. That frees the professional purchasers to spend their time improving relationships with suppliers and negotiating terms for buying goods and services.

One-quarter of US corporate purchasing managers say their companies will move MRO procurement to the Net by 1999, according to a survey released by distributor W.W. Grainger, Inc.[1] As discussed in Chapter 3, there are various methods used to move non-production buys to the Internet. Some companies are buying directly from their vendors' Web sites; others are developing their own intranet buying sites that incorporate electronic catalogs from many vendors.[2]

Vendors are Working to Improve Their Catalog Ordering Process

Managing catalog content is becoming a major sore point for IT as massive challenges face on-line sellers. Not only do they have to develop an information repository and infrastructure to manage their own data, they have to establish procedures to publish that catalog data--often with urgent demands for customization--to an ever-increasing number of locations.

For users like supply powerhouse W.W. Grainger, the e-commerce mandate remains clear: "The easier you make it for customers to do business with you, the more orders you're going to get," says Daniel Hamburger, president of Grainger Internet Commerce. "You've got to be able to provide buy-side content if that's what the customer wants. You have to provide a direct-access Web site, and you have to be on every virtual desktop by working with the software players."

But, he added, "That strategy is not for the meek, and it calls for a tremendous investment." WW Grainger has aimed much of that investment at its product information, which it views as "a key strategic asset," Hamburger says. That includes dedicating a group inside the company specifically to manage product information and building a common information repository--residing in an Oracle database and managed via a variety of management tools from Requisite and other vendors--to enable the publishing of catalogs to any format, he adds.[1]

Exhibit 9-1 provides a list of buying activities and case studies which are presented in this chapter.

Exhibit 9-1 - Summary of Non-Production Buying Case Studies

Buying Activity	Case Study
Multiple Catalogs	Raytheon
Non-Production Purchases	UPS Fijitsu
Low Dollar routine purchases	Master Card Honeywell
Tracking shipments	Manitoulin
Automated purchasing system	Xerox
Automating manual purchasing	City of Las Vegas
Office Supplies	Canadian Imperial Bank
MRO Buying	Morgan Stanley Dean Witter & Company
Small-business buying	Best of Italy -- Retail
Buying Electronic Distribution	Allied Electronics
School Buying	School Specialty Inc.

Raytheon -- Multiple catalogs and suppliers

Problem: Needed a system to incorporate catalogs from multiple suppliers and provide a consistent and intuitive look and feel for multiple users.

Solution: Raytheon built a site on its intranet for employees to buy supplies ranging from electrical and computer parts to maintenance and office supplies. The site was developed with the help of Tradex's Electronic Commerce Systems, Inc., located in Tampa, Fla. The system incorporates catalogs from about 50 suppliers and gives Raytheon employees, who range from scientists and lab technicians to maintenance people and secretaries, a consistent and intuitive look and feel to save from having to learn 50 ways of navigating.

The site includes products that only Raytheon employees are authorized to buy, with pricing and terms as negotiated with Raytheon. The site is customized further for each department and each person in each department. For example, a user who needs electronic items can access parts of the intranet that list items such as memory boards and software. A user who purchases only offices supplies does not have access to the electronic-items part of the intranet. Similarly, each user screen shows only those features that user is authorized to access.[3]

UPS -- Non-production Purchases

Problem: Better management of the $10.6 billion a year it spends on non-production purchases for its 360,000 employees was needed.

Solution: UPS turned to Oracle Strategic Procurement Applications to streamline its purchases and gain an improved understanding of its 70,000 suppliers. It also helped UPS realize economies of scale with selected suppliers that were not achieved prior to system implementation.

Results: While only 13,000 users are currently on the system, it has already reduced its payables and purchasing processing time by 25% or 10 hours per person per week. Each business day the system is receiving over 180,000 hits.[3]

Fijitsu -- Non-production Purchases

Problem: The need to better leverage non-production purchases.

Solution: Fijitsu, a manufacturer of disk drives and other components, uses ProcureWorks, procurement software from RightWorks Corp., for 350 of its 700 employees who purchase several million dollars' worth of non-production supplies annually. Currently this accounts for only a fraction of Fujitsu's 15,000 employees in the United States. Meanwhile, at the company's other divisions, employees are using different procurement applications. The new ProcureWorks system will allow Fujitsu Computer Products of America employees to download product information into ProcureWorks from MarketSite.net, and collaborate with other Fujitsu divisions to gain more leverage and negotiate better prices with suppliers.

Results: The ultimate objective of Fujitsu's plans are to negotiate single contracts on items such as mobile and data communications, travel, and perhaps even consulting services, which would help the company realize considerable savings.

MasterCard -- Low-dollar Purchases

Problem: Efficient process needed for low-dollar routine purchases and data connections between buy-side procurement systems and payment products such as corporate credit cards.

Solution: MasterCard International, Inc.'s Corporate Purchasing Card, or P-Card, works like a credit card but is used for employee purchases. MasterCard is building an Internet gateway that will connect procurement applications with supplier systems and provide the missing data to allow linkages to buy-side sites and credit-card payment. It is appropriately called MasterCard Commercial Card Gateway.

Results: This system will help streamline buying and deliver authorization and tracking reports to purchasing departments. Integrating those reports will give users a complete record of corporate purchasing activities and enable integration between individual cardholder reconciliation procedures and general-ledger accounting requirements.[4]

Honeywell -- Low-dollar Purchases

Problem: Honeywell, Inc. (which recently merged with Allied-Signal Corporation), is an $8+ billion-dollar global leader in control technology with more than 50,000 employees in 95 countries. Keeping track of who was buying what, from whom, and at what price had become an impossible task.

Solution: Honeywell began using Oracle Strategic Procurement, a fully automated Internet-based software suite that supports many types of purchases. "The Honeywell Mall" is an electronic marketplace at Honeywell's corporate office where users can find and order everything from office supplies to temporary personnel from on-line catalogs at pre-negotiated prices--directly from their desktops--24 hours a day, 7 days a week.

The system removed the manual processes usually associated with these types of purchases and replaced them with a streamlined, decentralized electronic-commerce solution. One set of business processes drives the entire process, ensuring consistency across the enterprise. The system allows buyers to see the price, quality, and delivery information for all purchases across all locations. This system provides Honeywell's corporate buyers with the key information on volumes by location, enabling them to use their buying power more wisely and to negotiate supplier contracts with major cost savings.

Results: In addition to cost savings, the system's speed enables reduced cycle time, which improves response to customers. User self-service allows users to place orders directly under contract with suppliers. This action has made the purchasing cycle simpler and faster because it eliminates redundancies by giving release authority to users. When employees enter requests themselves, it eliminates the need for double entry by the purchasing department. For self-service to be effective, employees must have access to on-line catalogs with the content they need, with a powerful search engine so they can actually find the times they need to buy from the right supplier at the negotiated price. For purchasing, the amount of information enables them to manage their supplier base much more strategically.[5]

Manitoulin -- Tracking Shipments

Problem: Manitoulin had an old shipment-tracking system that was slow and unwieldy. Customers would call Manitoulin's customer service representatives directly. The representatives would then track a shipment and either fax or phone back a status report. The process could take anywhere from 12 hours to two days. The company wanted a system that was cost-effective, easy to operate, available 24 hours a day, and extremely secure.

Solution: Using IBM's Net.Data on an AS/400, customers are now able to track their cargo via an on-line form. Information can be password-protected. Customers can also e-mail requests and receive answers within thirty minutes. Manitoulin plans to continue to update this system by offering price quotes, pickup requests, and on-line proof of delivery.

Results: Since the site began operation in the fall of 1997, response from customers has been tremendous. Some have even chosen Manitoulin products solely because of the company's electronic tracking capabilities. Sales representatives have brought in new business by enticing customers with this new, value-added service. Finally, Manitoulin has been able to automate customer support while significantly lowering administrative costs.[6]

Xerox -- Complete Automated Purchasing System

Problem: Worldwide operations relied on manual and fragmented IT processes that limited their ability to leverage buying power. Xerox realized they had 50 stray systems, 100 planning systems, 100 different supplier acquisition systems, 50 build systems, 50 configure systems, 50 inventory systems, and 150 material-move systems.

Solution: Xerox moved these systems into a common integrated suite of ERP applications, including Internet-based tools, to support its worldwide operations. Xerox wanted a long-range partner with major global presence. Xerox selected Oracle. "Oracle is the first and only vendor to create a procurement solution that enables a company to consolidate all purchasing activities into a single solution, regardless of industry size or type of purchasing," says Kevin Miller, senior director of Oracle applications.

Xerox selected Oracle Strategic Procurement, a fully automated, Internet-based software suite, for its purchasing efforts. The tool overcomes information deficits by capturing important data. The overall results of implementing such a system are listed in Exhibit 8-2. It also provides the ability to track savings opportunities by automatically analyzing trends, organizational spending, and supplier performance. Finally, it can also help find and manage the best suppliers by providing the necessary information to help create, manage, and leverage supplier contacts more effectively. Requests for quotations are posted on the Internet for new and existing suppliers to respond to. And suppliers can see how well they are performing in terms of meeting delivery performance and shipping schedules.[7]

Exhibit 8-2 - Purchasing Improvement Due to e-Purchasing

Results	Before	After
Cycle time -- request for payment	days, weeks	hours
Order accuracy	less than 50%	greater than 99%
Percent of purchases under approved contracts	less than 30%	greater than 80%
Processing cost per purchase order	$150.00	$25.00

City of Las Vegas -- Transforming a Manual Purchasing System

Problem: Incorporated in 1905 as a railroad town with 800 inhabitants, the City of Las Vegas expects to serve about 2 million people in the Las Vegas Valley by 2005. It needed to transform its manual purchasing system.

Solution: Implement Oracle's Purchasing application system.

Results: It completely transformed the city's manual business processes, providing an electronic communications framework for Las Vegas' daily procurement activities. Employees migrated from submitting requests for goods and services on paper to inputting the requisitions on line, reducing paper handling and time expenditure. The Purchasing staff now automatically creates purchase orders from these electronic requisitions; the city purchases the items; employees receive them; and Oracle Payables pays the invoices, which are then posted to Oracle General Ledger.[7]

Canadian Imperial Bank of Commerce -- Office Supplies

Problem: CIBC presently spends $1.2 billion a year on

office supplies and services. With 1,400 retail branches in Canada and close to 100 more investment offices worldwide. Many banks like CIBC are concerned about cost management.

Solution: Use Ariba.com technologies.

Results: CIBC is counting on the Internet-based electronic procurement system from Ariba Technologies to save at least $33 million annually and is shooting for 15% savings.[8]

Morgan Stanley Dean Witter & Co. -- MRO Supplies

Problem: Implement a Web-based procurement system for MRO and office supplies.

Solution: This $31 billion financial services company hopes to have its 10,000 U.S. employees in 500 locations buying supplies on line by the end of 1999. It plans to roll out its on line system in Europe and Asia in mid-2000.

Morgan Stanley retained Deloitte Consulting's DRT Systems unit to validate vendor claims about their systems' capabilities. The results indicted that the vendors had a lot of technology expertise, but frequently didn't know much about purchasing..

Another financial firm, T. Rowe Price, Inc., recently began the first phase of its Web-procurement initiative using American Tech, Inc.'s PurchasingNet SQL application and CatalogJunction middleware. T. Rowe Price will test the system with 200 IT employees buying IT products, and plans a full-scale rollout to 4,000 users buying all supplies by August, 2000.[9]

Best-of-Italy -- Small Business Buying

Problem: Best-of-Italy is an on-line retailer that wanted to build a mall site to provide connectivity, services, and visibility for its suppliers' various product offerings. Their strategy was to enable new suppliers to rent space easily on Best-of-Italy's website, thus suppliers wouldn't have to create their own websites. The Best-of-Italy mall also had to enable secure, on-line payments.

Solution: Best-of-Italy built their e-Commerce site using

IBM's Net.Commerce solution. Since all the development work had been done by IBM, the Net.Commerce solution made it easy for Best-of-Italy to construct the site and update it frequently as new shops joined the mall. This allowed them to dedicate more resources to their customers and to streamline their own business operations. And the encryption technology incorporated in IBM's Net.Commerce ensured the complete security of customer personal data.

Results: For individual suppliers participating in the Best-of-Italy on-line mall, the benefits of the "Best of Italy" site are clear. They establish an on-line presence without investing in their own solutions. For Best-of-Italy, the benefits are equally clear: the IBM solution relieves them of the burden of developing and innovating the site's technology. And for customers, every aspect of the transaction is handled by Best-of-Italy, so they get the low prices and reliability they are accustomed to as Best-of-Italy customers.[10]

Allied Electronics, Inc. -- Electronic Distribution Buying

Problem: Efficient method needed for purchasing small quantities of leading-edge Research-and-Development (R&D) type products.

Solution: The $160 million catalog business of Allied Electronics, Inc., is playing an increasingly important role in the R&D side of the business, by targeting engineers and purchasers involved in new-product development. Formerly relegated to the MRO (maintenance, repair, and operations) market, catalogs are increasingly being used for sourcing small quantities of leading-edge products. Engineers now place about 30% of Allied's total incoming orders, with traditional purchasing departments accounting for the remaining 70%. Of the 700,000 catalogs that Allied mails annually, more than half are distributed to engineers, and a growing number of Allied's customers have been allowing engineers instead of purchasers to buy products, according to Ed Bridges, senior vice president of sales for Allied Electronic's located in Fort Worth, Texas.

"The cost of [processing] a normal purchase order is roughly $60, whereas if an engineer places an order [via] procurement card or credit card, it cuts the cost by 50%, particularly if it's for a small-item purchase," he says.

Although catalogs are still Allied's biggest marketing tool, the company has seen a surge in CD-ROM and Internet usage, says Art Pierard, Allied's senior vice president of product marketing.

Results: The company launched its Web site (www.allied.avnet.com) three years ago. In early 1999, the site averaged 8,000 hits daily. Roughly 3% of Allied's sales come from Internet orders, according to Bridges. "About 5% of these hits will turn into orders," he says.[11]

School Specialty, Inç. -- School Buying

Problem: How to allow teachers and school administrators to buy products on line?

Solution: School Specialty, Inc., a distributor of educational products, has created a portal with an electronic-commerce component to allow teachers and school administrators buy products on line, and also meet in chat rooms to discuss lesson plans or swap ideas for improving student/teacher interaction.

School Specialty turned to systems integrator Proxicom, Inc., of Reston, Va., to devise a system that will help make computers not only a classroom tool, but also a way to facilitate procurement of everything from desks to microscopes to blackboard erasers.

"[With School Specialty] we're doing e-commerce on business-to-business and business-to-consumer levels," says Steve Davies, director of Proxicom's retail and manufacturing practice. "Teachers and administrators will come in as part of the school system to enter orders. Teachers also spend money on their own for their classrooms, and they want to do more browsing [for products]." The Web site established for this activity is www.ClassroomDirect.com.

Once users have logged on to the system with valid passwords, intelligent agents will be able to identify users and determine their relative level of approval to make purchases. Users affiliated with particular school districts will view tailored pricing schemes based on both the quantity of products ordered by the district annually and attendant discounts, says Mike Beck, vice president and general manager of Proxicom's retail and manufacturing practice. Each district negotiates an individual contract with School Specialty. [12]

References

[1] Clinton Wilder, "Top of The Drug Firm Shifts Procurement To The Net -- But Buying Specs Meet Skepticism", Information Week November 17, 1997, Issue 657.

[2]Kathleen Melymuka, "What do Web buyers want?", Computer World, October 26, 1998.

[3]Kathleen Melymuka, "What do Web buyers want?", Computer World, October 26, 1998.

[4]Richard Karpinski, "Electronic Commerce Payment Gateway Powered By Java", Internet Week, April 12, 1999, Issue 760.

[5]Oracle advertising in Fortune, May 24, 1999.

[6]IBM Web page.

[7]Oracle advertising in Fortune, May 24, 1999.

[8]Oracle Web page: Oracle at Work with the City of Las Vegas.

[9]Clinton Wilder, "Top Of The Week; Morgan Stanley Joins Online Procurement Push -- System Could Handle Buying For 10,000 US Employees", Information Week, April 19, 1999, Issue 730.

[10]IBM Web page.

[11]EBN April 19, 1999, Issue1156, Section: Distribution.

[12]Amy Rogers, "Internetworking; Distributor Learns Valuable Lesson About E-Commerce", Computer Reseller News, April 05, 1999, Issue 836.

10
Lessons learned Implementing e-Purchasing *plus*

Implementing e-Purchasing *plus* requires a disciplined approach; not all organizations will be successful with their first attempt at implementing it. This chapter outlines some of the lessons that can help provide a smoother transition for successful implementation. These lessons have been learned via observation and experience.

Lessons learned can be categorized broadly in the following areas:

1. Commitment: Organization's commitment of capital, visibility, and priorities compared to other projects
2. Objectives: Clear understanding of the organization's objectives and how the e-Purchasing program will support and further the organization's objectives.
3. People: The selection of the right mix of people for the e-Purchasing team and the dynamics of people who will be working together on these activities.
4. Planning: Planning is the process whereby an organization

153

determines in advance what should be done to achieve its e-Purchasing goals. Plans should include financial and human resources as well as implementation timetables.

5. e-Purchasing *plus* "-isms": While the exact system to be used will evolve with the organization's goals and user objectives, a strong direction statement needs to be in place so individuals have a basic framework to strive for. These e-Purchasing *plus* -isms are some general rules to keep in mind during the implementation process.

Commitment

If an organization and its top management are not committed to the project they will never get the necessary resources and support needed for success. In other words, commitment is the single most important factor in positively impacting time and budget estimates. The implementation team needs continually to attempt to assess the degree of commitment through management actions and words. Look for these generic levels of commitment:

• Totally committed - "We will get it done come hell or high water." Such an attitude indicates that the implementation team will have room to maneuver with resources available to get the job done.

• Generally committed -- "It's the right thing to do and the timing is right." With this attitude the implementation team is more limited in what it can do since time may be a critical factor. If successes aren't forthcoming quickly management may lose interest in the project.

• In agreement -- "We'll monitor the situation and keep it in mind." This attitude means little support and resources and probably a timetable that sees interest increasing after a major event. These major events may include adoption by the firm's competitors or customers. Thus champions of e-Purchasing need to keep monitoring the actions of competitors.

• Wary -- "We will keep a close eye on it." Very little

resources and support for the project will be forthcoming. Under this scenario the e-Purchasing team should set small achievable goals that will show early success and perhaps prompt greater support. For example, a firm in this environment might want to begin using the Internet for placing limited low-dollar items that would win user support and generate savings.

• Edgy -- "One false step and we will pull the plug on this project." The e-Purchasing team will have to fight and scrap for every resource every step of the way and one problem will doom the project. In this environment it is very unlikely that any progress will be made. The team should look into using seller sites such as Grainger to take very small steps to further the program.

In summary, it is important to get high-level-executive understanding, consensus, commitment, and ongoing support. Second, obtain commitment and buy in at all levels. As a final caveat it is wise to assess the organization's environment and attitude toward e-Purchasing. An organization should not consider implementing these projects if it has upper management who feel these technologies are a passing fad and not a basic change in the business model. Also these programs are not for those looking for a quick fix or a way to heal a non-performing purchasing department.

Objectives

Objectives and goals are desired results toward which human activities are directed. Organizations depend on their people to carry out these goals and objectives. E-Purchasing goals need to be established in as specific and measurable terms as possible. These goals can be stated or official but should be ones in which behavior is directed toward these goals. Extending these goals to suppliers will in many cases require that purchasers treat suppliers, like customers. E-Purchasing will mean that changes in the suppliers organization and objectives must be developed for interaction with them. Thus one objective is to help suppliers so they can be better prepared to service you. The e-Purchasing team might want to remember the two basic rules of customer satisfaction. Rule number 1: "Remember--the customer is king." Rule number 2: "Revisit rule number 1." These objectives will also apply to objectives established for purchasing's internal customers.

In summary, develop and write down clear, concise, compelling strategic business imperatives, which then will be converted into specific objectives for your e-Purchasing efforts. For example, one firm established a strategic objective to have at least 75% of its total purchase expenditures over its secure extranet site. The objectives included surveying consultants and third-party providers as well as an implementation timetable for the selected system. These objectives were linked to other strategic initiatives in the firm, which included how to improve responsiveness to customers without raising inventories.

People and Organization

Once the commitment is obtained and general objectives are established, getting the best people with the necessary skills assigned to the e-Purchasing project becomes critical to success. The "champion" of the project needs to have an idea and even interview potential members of the team. It is important not to underestimate the importance of selecting the right team. Everyone may want to be on the team since it will have a very high profile and impact the basic operating process of the organization. The key is to select the right people and not overpopulate the team; it will have to be flexible and make key decisions as necessary. A checklist to help handle the e-Purchasing *plus* people issues is listed below:

- Develop a team format for the overall organization that has enough autonomy and top-management backing to make key decisions.
- Assign dedicated business resources to project.
- Put the best people on the project full time.
- Full time does not mean "the first 40 hours of a person's

work week." It means seeing the project through to completion. In some cases this may mean relieving the individuals temporarily from their current job responsibilities.
- Don't accept the people who are "available." Look for and interview those who have the necessary skills and experience and attitude.
- Back-fill with other employees or contractors/consultants.
- Don't let KEY people go too soon.
- Determine IT resources needed and then double them.
- Understand the types of people who are on the project and how to deal with them:

The team will encounter various types of people within the organization. It is important to recognize some general attributes. The list below categories 4 types of people.

1. Propellers -- Fast trackers who are sought out by everyone in the organization. You should challenge these individuals by assigning them to handle critical issues. You will have to make sure that they don't move too quickly without considering all the necessary alternatives.

2. Passengers -- These individuals are mostly along for the ride. They are not self-motivated and will probably not contribute a great deal. However they may serve as a "devil's advocate" by forcing you to consider some of the downside potential. On the dark side, you may have to watch them, as they could derail or sidetrack the project.

3. Boat anchors -- These individuals take one position, then dig in and will not change no matter what actions or facts are shown to them. Some early successes may move them to reconsider their positions ever so slightly. Usually they are defending either a small change or the "status quo," due either to their lack of understanding or fear of job change or loss. Ways to deal with "boat anchors" include changing their positions or getting them assigned to other

projects.

    4. Torpedoes -- These individuals are doing whatever they can by waiting to kill the project at any time. It may not be apparent in their words, but often it is in their actions or what you hear from others about their actions. Obviously you need to turn them over or reassign them. A discussion with them about their interests in the project, and then assignment to another one they do support, may be the best action.

    Once you have the people, you will need to decide on the team organization. e-Purchasing *plus* is a new dynamic area, and some important **considerations** and **ideas** about the organization and reward systems are listed below.

- Get everyone *comfortable* with matrix management. Matrix management means that the team may report to multiple managers. Everyone on the team should be aware of the potential for conflict, as e-Purchasing affects several functional areas.
- *Pioneers and or champions* are the ones with arrows in their backs. These individuals have borne and will bear much of the load and the attendant criticisms the program receives. Their belief in the necessity of the program keeps them moving forward in spite of the criticism. Given their reputation and perhaps the adversaries they have picked up they may not be the best leaders for the team.
- Assign people who *help with solutions* to key positions. These individuals take the attitude of lead, follow, or get out of the way.
- Minimize *diversion of key personnel* on task forces and new studies. Key personnel need to remain focused on moving the project forward and keeping the team on a timetable.
- Establish the *roles and responsibilities* of all team members. The specific organization established and the objectives will lead to the establishment of roles and responsibilities.
- Establish *project-team performance* measurements. As mentioned earlier, objectives must be measurable so that perfor-

mance is measurable.

• Provide *incentives* for key performers. One of the key issues will be deciding how to reward the team members. Will they be rewarded as a team or through their respective functional areas? These incentives can be monetary or recognition through awards and publicity.

• Transfer project-team members back to the *user community*. The goal of the projects requires a high amount of agreement from users. It is important that the team members report back to users the progress and decisions made in the e-Purchasing system. It is also important that members bring back user concerns and explain them.

• Talk *to end-users* up front in order to obtain "*buy in*" for the project. What items do they like and what would they like to see changed? Explain why the changes are being made. This will serve to reduce resistance to the program. Three major issues need to be addressed with users:

> 1) Do they fear that new technology will decrease their job security?
>
> 2) Are they comfortable with the current system?
>
> 3) Have users had previous bad experiences with IT deliveries?

Certain techniques have been used to overcome user resistance to new technologies. These include: 1) Training users just before implementation. Training done months before will result from loss of knowledge between the training and implementation time. 2) Offer learning incentives to users, such as increased budget for other training they may desire. 3) Deliver system in modules that are manageable learning units. This modular approach will insure that users aren't overwhelmed. 4) Involve users in decision making. Involvement has been shown to increase commitment to a decision.

Planning

The planning process sets the table for the activities that will occur. Plans should be revised or modified if the original plan falls short of the overall objectives. The biggest mistake made in e-Purchasing settings is forgetting the plan and moving on an "ad hoc" basis. This is an easy trap to fall into since this area of e-Purchasing is changing daily. Thus continual plan changes will be necessary in this arena. To maintain focus on the plan a consideration should be given to the issues listed below.

- Do *90% solution*. Getting 90 percent of a solution is much better than striving for 100% and not moving forward at all.
- Don't let the "*bells and whistles*" ruin the timetable. Focus on the basic objectives and not some of the add-ons that may be proposed by software providers or consultants.
- Use *business-driven vs. technology* driven implementation. When technology is the focus organizations become enamored with the level of technology and forget that technology is being employed to improve a process, not impress the IT manager.
- Organize by *business process*. E-Purchasing will affect many processes, and this is where the focus needs to be applied.
- Organize for *continuous improvement*. The first solution is not the final solution. The team must realize it will be continually updated and refined with experience.
- Integrate *like businesses and processes*. When implementing e-Purchasing across a multidivisional organization it is important to look for similar businesses to realize synergies.
- *Change processes*, business practices, and business policies instead of changing functionality of purchased software. As stated several times in this text, one of the keys to e-Purchasing is changing and re-engineering business processes.
- Focus on business-process *simplification*. Simple solutions can create dramatic improvements, so keep things basic.
- Develop *corporate-wide standards* and direction in key

areas. This will provide a blueprint for those who follow and later adopters will not have to reinvent the process.

- Strive for *common technical implementation* worldwide. The benefits of common worldwide implementation will catch the attention of upper management.
- If it doesn't get *measured*, it doesn't get done. People are smart enough to comprehend what is important and how it will affect their standards of living.
- Remember--it's O.K. to make a "*mistake*." Mistakes will be made and need to be tolerated and not allowed to erode support for the project.
- Don't make *assumptions* about the end-user. Talk with him, interview him, and get his input. Otherwise several roadblocks may appear down the road.
- Web-based applications development is much *faster* than the testing.
- *International implementation* requires early involvement of representatives from each area. The reality is that suppliers in different parts of the world do not welcome or react to these tools the same way Americans do.
- *Involve suppliers early*. Like users suppliers are a key to e-Purchasing.
- Define *scope and stick* to it to get early success. Distinguish between must-haves and wants in your e-Purchasing project. This will enable you to implement the major part of the project earlier. You can "go live" with the other areas in a later phase of the project.
- Manage the project as an *investment*, and prioritize the sub-projects according to the payback they will provide the organization.
- Document a *training-and-education strategy*. This will involve the people who will receive training, the schedule, and the delivery.
- Establish *procedures* for quick issue resolution. Getting bogged down in minor details of this rapidly changing area will lead

to lowered motivation and interest levels by the team participants.

• Provide for slow decision-making on *major issues*. This may appear contrary to the previous issue. However, big decisions such as the type of system and software require input from many constituencies.

• Have a *clear understanding* of the e-Purchasing terms and capture them in written form. Without such a framework many hours are wasted arguing over terms if this agreement is not achieved. There are many good sources that can serve as a starting point for getting agreement on definitions.

• Plan for *post-implementation support* and more re-engineering upon completing the project.

• If possible *implement* e-Purchasing *plus* during a time of low business volume. People have more time and will devote a higher priority to the project during such slack periods.

• Have *post-implementation* support for at least six months after you go live. This will give users and suppliers a "safety net" to rely on for various questions and problems experienced in the early phases.

e-Purchasing *plus* "-isms"

When going through the implementation of an e-Purchasing *plus* implementation scenario, several "-isms" may keep you on track toward successfully reaching the goal. These include:

• e-Purchasing is more than the Internet.

• Pepper the organization with e-Purchasing "gees." For example, "Gee, do you know how much we will save and how quickly we can get those orders to our suppliers?!"

• Understand ERP and the impact it will have on your business, or become a "dinosaur."

• Remember--when striving to implement e-Purchasing *plus*, it's O.K. to make a "mistake."

• Change processes, business practices, and business policies instead of changing functionality of purchased software.

- Don't be a roadblock to solutions. On the contrary, help with solutions by leading when appropriate, following when necessary, or getting out of the way when you are blocking progress.
- Always practice M.B.W.A.(Management By Wandering Around). Find out what is really going on by being in the location where the activity is occurring. Don't stay in your office and rely on feedback.
- ERP will help your organization move more quickly toward an e-commerce environment.
- Involve suppliers early in the program. They will have to live with the program, so make it easy for them to use and adopt.
- Peoples' attitudes need to resemble Colombo's (methodical problem solvers), not Superman's (those who want to move mountains).
- People who behave as "Propellers" will provide the best chance for the success of e-Purchasing & ERP programs.
- Look for a 90% solution not perfection.
- Understand the two rules for customer satisfaction:
    - Rule Number 1: The Customer is King.
    - Rule Number 2: Revisit Rule Number 1.
- Treat suppliers like customers. Service them so they can be better prepared to service you.

These lessons are certainly not a cure-all for e-Purchasing *plus* but they will lead your organization in the right direction, since the rules have been proven to work in other environments. Keep these lessons in mind as you move through the tough days of the implementation phase.

Section 3

ERP Systems & e-Purchasing *plus* Solution Providers

11
ERP Software
Vision & Reality

The ERP portion of the overall e-Purchasing *plus* strategy is usually a major portion of the entire implementation.

SAP is the leading software vendor in the ERP business. The company has a 41% market share worldwide and over 250,000 users around the world at over 19,000 customer sites.

SAP's literature states that its ERP software "is the complete solution for all business functions within a business enterprise; it integrates related business tasks and its ease of domestic as well as international implementation is well known."

Benefits & Problems with SAP

Customer statements about SAP's ERP software systems as stated in its sales literature are (as expected) very complimentary. They include the following comments:
- allows us to become an industry leader, not a follower
- selected SAP because it reflects, industry-wide, best financial business practices
- it is a catalyst to redesign our business model

167

- we wanted a system that would change as our business changed
- we needed to maintain control and speed internal processes
- lets us make more efficient use of information as a production factor [1]

As with any system or product there are also detractors who cite problems with SAP's software. The majority of these concerns focus on problems associated with implementing SAP and the costs.

On the other hand, there is a lot of "press" about the problems associated with implementing SAP.

- impossible to implement: as of 1999, only 58% of SAP projects initiated in 1992 are in production
- configuring nightmares
- requires company consensus
- exorbitant to implement: only 26% of these projects were finished on time and within budget
- high cost of consulting
- hidden costs difficult to identify
- too rigidly structured: imposes its own methods of working
- average project requires 2.5 years from initiation to achieve ROI[2]

Many of the above concerns relate to the fact that these organizations felt their ERP systems failed. Michael Donovan, president of R. Michael Donovan & Co., Inc., states that there are a few ERP showcase companies, but it is more common to find executives very frustrated by the SAP experience.

ERP failure is defined as having systems that are installed but really not implemented: the software is running but the system is not fully utilized because data inaccuracies make the information almost useless; poorly educated and trained users cannot effectively use the system and often go outside the system to get their jobs done; or business processes that are intended to be solved by the ERP system are flawed and result in the errors being created faster and no solutions.

Deployment Strategy

Deployment of an ERP package is typically performed on the basis of organizational structure. The two major types of organization for those that have multiple products and multiple business units are 1)structured decentralization or 2) geographic location. The following are highlights of the two different strategies.

Structured Decentralization Strategy

The major focus here is on deploying ERP on the basis of the individual business unit. Each business unit is its own integrated business. Examples of firms who extensively utilize the business unit model include Unilever, FMC, Polaroid, Hoerst. When your organization considers which category you fall into, look at the characteristics of structured decentralization. Such organizations tend to have the following characteristics:
1) autonomous business units are the norm; 2) each business unit has its own end-to-end business processes (marketing, sales, production, procurement, etc.); 3) the "business unit is king" in the organization and business-unit managers have a great deal of autonomy and are rewarded for their unit's financial performances; 4) financial consolidation and reporting are the major integrated portions of these highly decentralized units; 5) given these various independent units, the organization tends to be more IT-driven in order to achieve consolidation benefits, rather than business-re-engineering driven; 6) process re-engineering is adopted unevenly across the different business units.

Geographic Strategy

Deploying ERP in a firm that is grouped by geographic location is challenging. In this environment integration happens within a specific geographic unit. The focus of deployment efforts is the coordination within a particular geographic region. Examples of firms that organize along geographic lines include Hoffman LaRoche, Black & Decker, Elf, BASF, and BSM. Characteristics of these organizations include the existence of autonomous geographic units and the fact that each of these geographic units has its own end-to-end business processes of marketing, sales, production, purchasing, etc.

ERP/SAP Project Costs

A typical SAP implementation could cost from one to several million dollars, depending on how much re-engineering a company plans to do.

Common SAP-project cost allocation is as follows:

Project Management	10%
Project Planning	10%
Software	20%
Hardware	15%
Training	15%
Consulting	30%

Training Costs

The project team gets from two to four weeks of training. The first two weeks are spent in the classroom focusing on SAP in general; the cost for this is $750 to $3,000 per student, depending on what companies are selected to perform the actual training. At a later time another two weeks extending over several months are required. These workshops emphasize specific SAP functionality.

End users receive two weeks of classroom training, costing $500 to $1,500 per student. This training focuses on how the user interfaces with the system, the tasks that can be performed, and the information that can be captured.

Project Team

The typical SAP project team consists of the consultant group and the user or customer group. Typically there are one to two consultants assigned to each of the ERP modules listed above. The project-team ratio is usually four to five customer participants per consultant. The SAP consultant team size ranges from six to 15 in number. These consultants have specialized skills and fall into one or more of the following categories:

Project leader	1
Module/Process consultants	3-8
Basic technical consultants	1-2
ABAP (SAP Programmers)	1-4

The user or customer team consists of 30 to 75 people. These individuals come from various functional groups:

Project manager	1
Business process owners	4-8
Business process analysts	15-50
IT members	10-15

References

[1]SAP Sales Literature- R/3 in the Real World: Our Client's perspective
[2] 1999 Annual America's SAP User Group Conference, Dallas Texas

12
ERP - Realizing the Benefits

Although companies have been pouring billions of dollars into the implementation of Enterprise Resource Planning (ERP) systems, many have not done disciplined return-on-investment (ROI) analysis. Companies have had good business reasons for putting these analysis projects on hold, including integrating disparaged business units, consolidating redundant systems problems, and solving their year 2000 (Y2K) problems. Toro, a $1.1-billion maker of lawn mowers and snow throwers in Minneapolis, says its SAP implementation eliminated about 70 homegrown systems that would have required $12 to $15 million in Y2K remediation work.

In the aftermath of Y2K, companies are starting to generate hard numbers. Maybe its because the efforts of Y2K were completed and attention is being paid to the real numbers in these projects. So, how good are the returns? Meta Group surveyed 63 companies to determine what kind of payback, if any, they were getting from their ERP investments. It found that, over a five- to six-year period, the average company incurred a negative ROI of $1.5 million. Also, on average it took a company 23 months to get an ERP system up and running, at a cost of $10.6 million for the implementation and

173

another $2.1 million for annual systems maintenance.

In addition to the quantitative analysis, firms are asking hard questions as to whether ERP is enabling the accurate and timely execution of business plans and key decisions across the organization. ERP's role as a Decision Support System (DSS) involves taking key input from marketing, operations, suppliers and customers. Too many firms proceed rapidly into ERP implementation without considering the impact on these affected groups. At a strategic level, ERP should be driving the firm's business plans. At an operational level, Material Requirements Plans (MRP), warehousing, and distribution need to be analyzed for synergies and commonalties.

Further, looking externally out from an ERP system will involve the use of e-Purchasing. When reviewing these outside linkages it is important to remember that information flows have become a strategic weapon. Today rapid information flows will replace inventory and thus make the organization much more flexible in the competitive arena it operates in.

This rapid information transfer also is extended to the area of new-product development, involving both suppliers and customers early in the development stages. Thus e-Purchasing must be made part of and integrated into the organization's overall ERP efforts, for the strategic and operational decisions are greatly influenced by the efficient flows of information both upstream and downstream in the supply chain. Software suppliers are scrambling to develop end-to-end supply chain solutions that allow complete supply-chain linkages.

ERP System Expectations vs. Reality

Some analysts say that ERP may provide its greatest ROI potential as a platform for the next generation of e-Commerce and e-Business applications. Benchmarking Partners recently completed an ROI study involving 62 US companies that have invested in enterprise applications. The study identified several areas in which companies are likely to see payback. They include an overall reduction of IT costs, inventory reductions, improved cash management, reduction in personnel, and faster order management from the time a company receives an order to the time it ships the product.

But the differences between what companies expect and what they get can be significant. For example, 45% of companies anticipated benefits in personnel reduction, while only 34% said they actually saw such benefits. And while 25% anticipated an IT cost reduction, only 12% got it. On the flip side, only 18% of companies interviewed thought they would see improvement in order management, but a full 33% got that benefit, and while 12% anticipated a benefit in the financial close cycle (the time it takes a company to close a quarter), 20% achieved it.[1]

Benefits of ERP

Based on Benchmarking Partners' ongoing research of 350 ERP implementations, ERP benefits are broken into two areas.

1. Economic:

> Financial Management
> Personnel
> Reduction of Total IT Cost
> Inventory
> Supplier Mgmt/ Procurement
> Order Management

2. Strategic:

> Integration & Process
> Information
> Customer Responsiveness / Flexibility
> Cost/Productivity
> New Application Infrastructure

Robinson's 1997 article discusses several Enterprise Resource Planning system technologies. ERP employs client/server technology, meaning that a user's (client's) system runs an application (accounting, inventory management, etc.) that accesses information from a common database-management system (server). This system reflects the concept of decentralized computing.

The core of an ERP system is its common database, which interacts with all the applications in the system; it permits no redundancies in the data and integrity is ensured. There are the functional software packages for each individual business unit (finance, human resources, order processing) that are provided by each software supplier. Most ERP systems start with a set of core modules, and offer additional modules from which a company can choose. All of these applications are fully integrated to provide consistency and visibility for all the activities across entire operations. However, ERP systems require users to comply with the processes and procedures as described by the application.

In such a system, functional business units utilizing integrated applications and sharing a common database eliminate repetitive needs such as re-inputting data from one application to another. Time reductions are achieved by minimizing delays retrieving or disseminating information. Analyzing business decisions enterprise-wide results in time savings, improved control, and elimination of overlapping operations.[1]

After implementing ERP, Par Industries in Moline, Illinois, reduced lead time to customers from six to two weeks, delivery performance increased from 60% on time to more than 95%, work-in-progress inventory dropped almost 60% and the life of a shop floor order went from weeks to hours.

J.R. Simplot Co., a potato product manufacturer, recently achieved significant benefits at minimal cost from implementing an ERP system. Being a low-margin business, Simplot opted to run a trial ERP implementation. Within four months of initiation, the project went live. The trial was conducted for $100,000 including training costs. The benefits were achieved almost immediately: redundant paperwork was eliminated; control was improved through more rigorous lot control of their products; costs were reduced by more efficiently ordering packaging supplies; yield improved by more effectively scheduling to maximize raw-materials inventories. It is estimated that the trial paid back more than 400% of their original investment. (Robinson, 1997)

Concur Technologies' Web page discusses savings and provides comparisons of paper-based versus automated procurement systems. In a manual, paper-based system, the cost per requisition is $98, while it's $10 per purchase requisition for automated systems. Travel-and-entertainment expense management for a manual system is $36 per expense report, versus an automated system's $7.

Reference

[1]Robinson, Anne, "Enterprise Resource Planning" (December 14, 1997) http://mansci2.uwaterloo.ca/~msci604/summaries/erp.html

13
e-Purchasing *plus* Software Company Products

With recent advances in technology, it is becoming more convenient and much less difficult to be a participant in e-Purchasing *plus*. All purchasing organizations, regardless of size, need to explore the potential opportunities that new technology will offer for the on-line procurement of supplies and services. Many companies are now realizing the ease of use of e-Purchasing *plus* tools, and are putting their capital and marketing dollars behind projects to ensure that they reap the benefits associated with applying this technology in procurement. Meanwhile, e-Purchasing software suppliers are also jockeying for a share of the procurement business. Listed below are several software products and the companies that have developed e-purchasing applications. This list represents a "best effort" on the part of the authors to provide a representative list. The companies on this list are changing daily, so if we have inadvertently omitted any names, we encourage both purchasers and suppliers to contact us.

Exhibit 11-1 - e-Purchasing Companies & Products

<u>Company</u>	<u>Product</u>
Agentics	Supply Channel
American Software	ECON/Purchasing
Ariba	Operating Resource Management System (ORMS)
Aspect	eXplore 2000 -- eDesign, eSource, and eOperate
Baan	E-Enterprise suite
Brio	Brio ONE
BuyerZone	e-Catalog Central and Get a Quote.
Chemdex Corp	
Clarus	E-Procurement
Commerce One	BuySite 5.0
ConnectInc.com	MarketStream
Dazel	Web Delivery for Purchasing
Digital Market	Digital Buyer 5.0
Dun and Bradstreet & SAS Institute Inc.	
Elcom	PECOS Internet Procurement Manager
FairMarket	AuctionPlace, AutoMarkdown
Free Markets	Bid Ware Internet Technology
General Electric	TPNPost
Information Builders	WebFOCUS
Intelisys Electronic Commerce	4Sight Benchmark Procurement processes
Kewill ERP Division	MAX -Purchasing Control Module
Netscape	BuyerXpert
NetReg	Purchasing Online
Oracle	Fast Forward Internet Procurement (FFIP)
PartNET	eCommerce
Peoplesoft	Uses Commerce One Procurement products
Procureit	ProcureIT

Company	Product
ProcureNet	OneSourceProcurement
PurchasePro.com	PurchasePro.com
PurchasingCenter.com	None
Remedy	Remedy Purchasing@Work
SAP	SAP R/3; mySAP.com
SAS Institute	Supplier Relationship Management
SciQuest	Custom Purchasing Solutions
Solix	iOperations
Supplybase.inc	Supplybase.manager
SupplierMarket.com	SupplierMarket.com
Technical Services Associates	Gateway Client Server
Trilogy Software	Buying Chain
Works.com	Works.com

Company: Agentics
Product: SupplyChannel
Procurement application: According to Agentics' Web page, SupplyChannel enables employees to execute self-service procurement. Orders for approved goods from approved vendors are placed by employees directly from their desktops via the company's intranet. Full management control at all stages of the transaction is maintained. This process eliminates the buyer's need to maintain suppliers' product data.

SupplyChannel enables users simultaneously to access multiple on-line catalogs, residing at supplier sites, as though they were one, unified catalog. Suppliers do not need to provide any special or dedicated interface.[1]

Company: American Software
Product: ECON/Purchasing
Procurement application: According to American Software's Web

page, ECON/Purchasing provides real-time interactive links to add, update, and check purchase-order status on line. Gives requisitioners the power to create, update, and inquire about purchase orders and requisitions via the Internet.[2]

Company: Ariba
Product: Operating Resource Management System (ORMS)
Procurement application: According to Ariba, Inc.'s Web page, ORMS is an on-line marketplace managed by a third party where buyers and suppliers can establish relationships and conduct business. Many analysts believe that properly deployed trading communities offer the most economical and rewarding e-commerce solutions for buying organizations of all sizes.

Ariba houses and manages supplier catalog content and provides a litany of transaction and order-routing services to participating buyers and suppliers. Buyers receive order confirmations, transaction histories, and audit trails. Rounding out the community experience at Ariba.com is a series of nice-to-have features, in addition to the must-have communication and transaction-support capabilities. Participants also have access to industry news and events, interactive forums, supplier evaluation ratings, and informational libraries from Dun & Bradstreet and Hoovers.

Ariba sees Ariba.com as the first step of an evolutionary process. Their first priority is to connect multiple buyers with multiple sellers and enable seamless communication and transactions. Subsequent enhancements to the community will include vertical industry buying consortiums, auctions for surplus materials, and pre-negotiated supplier contracts.[3]

Company: Aspect
Product: eXplore 2000, which includes eDesign, eSource, and eOperate
Product Application: According to Aspect's Web page, eXplore enables collaboration between procurement, product development,

operations, and suppliers. This system is used to streamline inbound supply in product development, procurement, and plant operations, allowing companies to design products more efficiently and reduce the costs of procured parts and supplies.

eXplore 2000 has a universal Web client, enabling anyone with a standard Web browser to access the application. eXplore 2000 will be instantly intuitive to the user, with Web-style text search across multiple part properties, part classes displayed in Yahoo-like Web links, visual searches, forward and back commands and hyper links for navigation, and help text and drop-down menus and displays. The eXplore Web interface has been designed for the broad array of casual users that want straightforward access to parts, materials, and supplier information.

Similarly, eXplore 2000 supports collaboration with external supplier organizations through tools that exchange bills of materials or extract and update product data, requests for price quotes, information, or proposals.

eDesign will include all the current decision support capabilities of Aspect's Strategic Product Development solution, but will be accessible through Web clients. It will enable design organizations to create a central repository for all corporate part information, with parts dynamically ranked for preference based on corporate business rules. It will provide life-cycle management of parts and the ability to guide engineers to select components for new designs based not just on functional characteristics, but on business factors such as cost, supplier ratings, quality ratings, and a part's reuse potential.

eSource is the next generation of Aspect's Strategic Sourcing Management solution and will include the ability to do spend analysis on parts and supplies across the corporation, and to demand roll-ups, supplier analysis, and optimization reports using a Web browser client.

eOperate is the next generation of Aspect's Strategic Plant Management solution, designed to allow plant operations executives to optimize the procurement and use of MRO (maintenance, repair, and operations) goods, equipment spares, and tooling.[4]

Company: Baan
Product: E-Enterprise suite
Procurement application: According to Baan's Web page, E-Enterprise suite is designed to let users extend their Baan manufacturing, financial, and distribution software on the Web to collaborate better with customers, suppliers, and partners.

E-Enterprise consists of E-Sales, E-Procurement, and E-Collaboration. E-Sales lets users set up an on-line storefront that Baan says will be integrated with its back-office enterprise-resource planning applications. Also included is E-Config, a self-service product configurator that works over the Web.

E-Procurement lets companies quickly and easily purchase office supplies and production materials. It also sits on top of traditional Baan ERP applications and pulls out the operations and business information needed to execute a transaction.

E-Collaboration is a lower-cost alternative to electronic data interchange. It lets supply-chain partners share information such as contracts, purchase orders, and material forecasts over the Web. Data generated within the Baan ERP applications, such as a master production schedule or manufacturing diagrams, can be posted on a common site.[5]

Company: Brio
Product: Brio ONE
Procurement application: According to Brio's Web page, Brio ONE is comprised of the following.

1. Brio.Enterprise, an integrated suite of enterprise business intelligence tools for query, analysis, and analytical reporting across both client/server and Web environments. Brio.Enterprise graphical interface offers an intuitive environment for data exploration and decision making.

2. Brio.Report, a high-volume, high-performance server-based enterprise reporting environment is the only enterprise reporting solution with native access to over 125 combinations of databas-

es and operating environments. With Brio.Report, you can write reports anywhere, run them anywhere, and print them anywhere. It is specifically designed to handle high-volume reporting jobs, whether publishing information on a corporate intranet, processing production reports, or populating a data warehouse.

3. Brio.Portal is a Web portal for self-service access to any enterprise information no matter where it resides. Brio.Portal provides a Web-enabled solution to the problem of distributing business information by consolidating business intelligence objects (reports, documents, spreadsheets, data cubes, etc.) generated anywhere in the enterprise by any application and making them easily accessible, subject to security authorization, to non-technical users via standard browser technology. It allows users to run many types of business intelligence applications against any appropriate content.[6]

Company: BuyerZone
Product: e-Catalog Central and Get a Quote
Procurement application: According to Buyers Zone's Web page, Buyers Zone is a leading provider of purchasing advice and on-line shopping for small to mid-sized business. The site has over 75 buyer's guides on topics ranging from digital copiers to payroll services. In addition, there is access to helpful glossaries and resource centers.

Buyerzone has product database searches. Simply answer a few quick questions to zero in on the models or providers. It also has discussion forums. BuyersZone provides two methods to shop: e-Catalog Central and Get a Quote.

e-Catalog Central allows you to search multiple vendor catalogs, all at once, to find exactly what you need. You can also jump directly to the appropriate order form to place your purchase.

Get a Quote provides connection to a vendor that can offer service and support and get multiple quotes without picking up the phone.[7]

Company: Chemdex
Product: Offers a number of leading-edge solutions to scientists and enterprises
Procurement application: According to Chemdex's Web page, Chemdex offers a marketplace of hundreds of thousands of products, creation of multi-supplier orders, product search engines, contract pricing, customized supplier lists, approval work-flow functionality, enforcement of enterprise spending limits, and ordering guidelines. It also provides automated ordering, billing, tracking, shipping, reordering, summary billing, consolidated reporting, and ERP integration.[8]

Company: Clarus
Product: E-Procurement
Procurement application: Clarus' Web page describes a complete on-line purchasing system that does away with registration and per-transaction charges, for both buyers and sellers, on purchases run through its system. Instead, it charges buyers a flat $995 per month for unlimited transactions; that's in addition to enterprise license fees for its core e-procurement application. E-Procurement uses a shopping cart that makes buying easy and intuitive; little to no training is required. Employees view pictures and extended descriptions. And, it doesn't matter how many suppliers or catalog options are involved; the employee always sees the same view. No fees are charged to suppliers.

Clarus may charge fees for value-added services such as order tracking, inventory-level checks, and business-to-business auctions.[9]

Company: Commerce One
Product: BuySite 5.0
Procurement application: Commerce One's Web page describes BuySite 5.0 as on-line-procurement software that includes expense-reporting capabilities from Extensity, Inc., and data analysis tools from Cognos Corp. Cost is $2.5 million for unlimited users.

Company: ConnectInc.com
Product: MarketStream
Procurement application: According to ConnectInc.com's Web page, ConnectInc.com's MarketStream product is a full-spectrum e-commerce solution for developing state-of-the-art e-commerce. With MarketStream, Internet extensions to existing businesses or new net companies can create new e-business communities where multiple buyers and sellers come together under one roof.

Their application includes support for both the buy-side and sell-side of e-commerce transactions. MarketStream also includes support for the latest in Internet security and easy application configuration and administration. Other features are:

> Cross-supplier catalog search
> Product-specific attributes
> Customized pricing
> Buyer profiling and personalization
> Fulfillment tracking information
> Back-end system integration
> Robust reporting capabilities[10]

Company: Dazel
Product: Web Delivery for Purchasing
Procurement application: The system is a turnkey solution for delivery of purchase orders to suppliers on secure, private Web pages on your company's extranet. In addition, it provides e-mail notification of new deliveries and exception management reports to buyers. The solution provides immediate, verifiable Web delivery from the order cycle. For suppliers, the solution requires only a Web browser and e-mail.[11]

Company: Digital Market, Inc..
Product: Digital Buyer 5.0
Procurement application: According to Digital Market's Web page,

web procurement is an application that incorporates functions from Hewlett-Packard, Oracle, and Hyperion Solutions software.

Digital Buyer 5.0 offers performance and scalability with Oracle's Application Server, work-flow-management options based on HP's ChangeEngine, and supply-chain and return-on-investment analysis capabilities based on Hyperion's Essbase OLAP Server. The HP-powered Digital Buyer Workflow function includes modules for automating contract management, routing suppliers' alternative part suggestions, and updating supplier catalogs. Hyperion's Essbase is used for an add-on module for Digital Buyer Reporting and Analysis. Users will be able to analyze sourcing cycle times and cost-effectiveness by product, supplier, price, or region.[12]

Company: Dun and Bradstreet & SAS Institute Inc.
Procurement application: An enterprise procurement solution that consolidates transaction-level purchasing data and provides information about individual companies' procurement-spending totals.

Company: Elcom.com Inc.
Product: PECOS Internet Procurement Manager
Procurement application: Elcom's Web page indicates that PECOS Internet Procurement Manager requires of the customer only an Internet connection, Web browser, and internal e-mail client system.

Elcom has on-line access to over 56,000 products. Buyers have full order-entry and search capabilities, real-time order status and history, multiple search options, and electronic tracking of orders via hyperlinks to major carriers FedEx and UPS.

Elcom. electronic commerce software solutions provide a real-time link between the buyer and seller throughout product presentation, selection, ordering, fulfillment, and delivery. Elcom.com provides companies that have customer-controlled administration with the ability to route purchase lists for approval and creation of a customer-specific catalog with custom pricing and availability.[13]

<u>Company:</u> FairMarket
Product: AuctionPlace, AutoMarkdown
Procurement application: According to FairMarket?s web page, the FairMarket Network is an online auction network comprising some of the most widely recognized names on the Web. The FairMarket Network gives buyers and sellers a rich selection of auction resources without leaving the comfortable environment of their favorite portal site or e-commerce vendor.

AuctionPlace:

AuctionPlace is not a software package; it is a comprehensive solution that consists of implementation, hosting and support services for online auctions. Whether looking to build a community or expand e-commerce offerings, AuctionPlace creates a dynamic trading environment for buyers and sellers. AuctionPlace is easy to use. With this solution, companies work with FairMarket to deploy their own branded sites very rapidly, sometimes in a matter of days. The scalable technology is hosted and maintained on FairMarket systems, eliminating the need for customers to utilize any engineering or IT resources to develop and maintain their auction sites.

Buyer functionality includes: real time bidding with notification upon each change to bid status; auction agent for automatic bidding; searching by keyword; geography or product specification to locate listings; watch list to track specific auctions; auction clock to let bidders know remaining time on each auction listing; MyAccount area for personalized auction experience; email listing to a friend; a variety of formats: English, Dutch, Quick Win, Classifieds

Seller functionality includes:easy to post listings; ability to post large quantities at one time; several auction types or classifieds; unlimited text descriptions with option to use HTML; control auction start and end times; set reserve prices; automatic notification via email of winning bidder(s); image upload feature.

A site configuration module enables the user tomanage all aspects of the auction experience through a simple, web-based point and click interface. The module also provides robust reporting capabilities on all aspects of the auction site including bidding, listing and transaction activity. FairMarket also generates weekly WebTrends reports that include number of pageviews and in-depth traffic and auction site specifics.

AutoMarkdown:

AutoMarkdown is a clearance pricing mechanism typically used for selling multiple quantities of an item. It is the equivalent of repeated markdowns in the apparel industry or a department store clearance rack in which product prices decrease over time and buyers commit to purchase as soon as the price becomes attractive to them. As with all of their solutions, FairMarket provides services ranging from hosting to customer and end-user support, from technology implementation to the back-end management and reporting tools. Additionally, since participation requires registration, sellers gain valuable sales information for designing future programs. Buyers get immediate gratification and another exciting purchasing format.

If you've got overstock, this new auction format can help your business. AutoMarkdown is typically used for selling multiple quantities of an item. The mechanism is similar to repeated markdowns in the apparel industry or a department store clearance rack.

AutoMark works as follows: a merchant posts a group of items for an opening price of $80 per item. After 2 days, the price drops to $60 per item. After another 2 days, the price drops to $40 per item. The AutoMarkdowns continue until all items are purchased, the price hits the specified floor (designated by user), or the sale item runs out.[14]

Company: Free Markets
Product: BidWare® Internet technology
Procurement application: Conducts online auctions for industrial parts, raw materials, commodities and services. In these auctions, suppliers compete in real time for the purchase orders of large buy-

ing organizations by lowering their prices until the auction is closed. The Free Markets approach to creating successful online auctions involves blending a set of activities, information, and technology. The company insures that the the right bidders are present and prepared, works with buyers to select bidders to participate in each auction since as most buyers know not all suppliers are created equal.

Free Markets works with suppliers to insure they are clear about the products or services the buyer needs or the terms under which they are to be delivered. This includes both standard items and technically complex and custom-made ones. Working with several members of each client's purchasing organization to specify their needs in detail and communicate them to bidders before each auction is a key value added service provided by Free Markets. BidWare software was designed specifically to address the commercial needs of large industrial buyers.[15]

Company: General Electric
Product: TPNPost
Procurement application: According to GE's Web page, TPN is a sourcing tool to help businesses increase their purchasing productivity. TPNPost is an Internet-based solution that helps companies buy and sell products and services efficiently. This system enables buyers to select pre-qualified suppliers electronically from a global database; create and send Requests for Quote (RFQs) and drawings; receive, compare, and analyze bids in a single or multi-round bidding process; and notify all bidders of the results. It enables suppliers to publish their capabilities electronically in a global supplier database; receive RFQs; create and submit bids; and receive notifications regarding bidding status.

TPNPost is comprised of consulting services, desktop application software, on-line network services, community implementation services, and support services. Buyer functions include the following.

1. Buyers prepare RFQ information

2. Buyers identify potential suppliers
3. Buyers post RFQ to the Internet
4. Buyers invite suppliers to bid on the project
5. Suppliers download RFQ information from the TPN
6. Suppliers submit bids for each item in the project
7. Buyers evaluate the supplier bids and negotiate on line to achieve the "best deal"
8. Buyers accept the bid(s) that best meet their requirements

Buyers exercise their discretion to include the suppliers that best meet their requirements. Buyers search the TPN Post Community using several criteria, including SIC Code, industry, supplier name, supplier location, and DUNS number to locate companies that supply the particular service or commodity they are looking for. The buyer can then view a supplier's Registration Form to find more information about the organization. The buyer then evaluates suppliers based on the information provided and selects the suppliers he wants to include in an RFQ.

For suppliers, registration for GE TPN Post is FREE through 2000. Suppliers will get a user name, password, unlimited software upgrades, and the ability to receive and respond to an UNLIMITED number of RFQs until the end of 2000. Completing the registration form gives buyers a wealth of information about a supplier's company, including products, quality, and company history. Once a supplier joins TPN, buyers will be able to find it based on the information the supplier provides.

During the bidding process, suppliers cannot see each others' bids. After each round of bidding, the buyer sends status information regarding each item in the RFQ. The supplier will download the status information for the project. For each line item, the supplier will see a status of OPEN (indicating that the supplier is being invited to bid), ACCEPTED (supplier has won the business for that line item), BAFO (supplier is asked to bid one more time - Best And Final Offer), or CLOSED (supplier is not invited to bid on that line item).[16]

Company: Information Builders
Product: WebFOCUS
Procurement application: Information Builders' Web page indicates that it's product allows users to set up Web-based reporting systems with access to any data on any platform. These intranet and extranet applications deliver intelligent information to employees and partners.

WebFOCUS technology provides centralized reporting environments with ad hoc user analysis. It is capable of accessing any data anywhere -- including legacy and transactional data, plus packaged applications like SAP R/3. Portals enable every person within and beyond an organization to access the information he needs, no matter where it is.[17]

Company: Intelisys Electronic Commerce LLCe
Product: 4Sight
Procurement application: Intelisys's Web page describes 4Sight as a program that lets users of its IEC-Enterprise purchasing application compare their processes against a database of benchmarks from companies such as Cargill, Sprint, and TRW. Companies can use 4Sight to compare their process costs for purchasing non-production supplies to averages in the database, which is maintained by a unit of AnswerThink Consulting Group, Inc.[18]

Company: Kewill ERP Division
Product: MAX -- Purchasing Control Module
Procurement application: The Purchasing Control Module lets you create and print purchase orders, track purchased materials, maintain vendor information, and predict your cash requirements. This module also gives you information at your fingertips.

MAX displays MRP-generated orders and purchase requisitions in a spreadsheet grid. Users can select, maintain and auto-assign MRP generated orders to either new or existing POs, eliminating the need to use purchase requisitions, if desired. With extensive filtering and date range capabilities, MAX allows users select only the orders they want to view and customize the layout of the purchasing schedule grid based on their preferences. Problem orders are displayed in red and yellow for quick identification. Users can drill down on particular cells within the grid to view more detailed information. Require MRP generated requirements to be approved before assigning them to purchase orders. Flexible record selection criteria allows processing of bulk or specific orders.

Users can review POs by order number, vendor, part ID, blanket PO, or date range, and then open a PO by double-clicking a displayed order. The site displays inventory orders, non-inventory orders, or subcontract orders.

MAX uses the reporting tool, Crystal Reports as the engine for standard reports. All reports are customizable and have extensive sorting and filtering capabilities, giving access to information you need in the format you are used to.[19]

Company: Netscape
Product: Buyer Xpert
Procurement application: According to Netscape's Web page, BuyerXpert provides unified access to multiple local and remote supplier catalogs with drill-down, text, and attribute-search capabilities. Employees can quickly and easily find what they need from authorized vendors. Pertinent ordering information is automatically transferred to a requisition, virtually eliminating errors. A work-flow engine routes the requisition through the approval process based on the requisitioner, organizational structure, types of goods, spending limits, and other criteria as defined by the most powerful business rules found in any electronic-commerce application. E-mail notifications, approvals, automated reminders, and escalations help move purchase requisitions through the most complex of approval processes -- followed by automatic execution of the purchase order with a supplier of any size.

BuyerXpert supports the Open Buying on the Internet (OBI) standard, which allows buyers to access OBI-compliant supplier catalogs and selling systems. This reduces the administrative cost and overhead of maintaining product and pricing information in an internal catalog and enables the company to get its procurement application up and running quickly. BuyerXpert is able to execute transactions with a company's entire supply base, communicate with large suppliers using either existing EDI VANs or Internet EDI, and conduct business with smaller suppliers using Web forms and/or encrypted messaging. A supplier with access to the Internet or an e-mail address can participate in Internet commerce exchange, eliminating inefficient and expensive exchanges of faxes and phone calls.[20]

Company: NetReq
Product: Purchasing Online
Procurement application: NetReq's Web page describes PurchasingOnline as an Internet Site for connecting business and government professionals who buy and sell goods for their respective companies or organizations. A typical seller using PurchasingOnline works for a company that sells products to commercial businesses or governments in large or bulk quantities. The seller needs to be able to complete a significant number of responses-to-quote requests quickly and accurately to increase the chances of having successful quote responses. The seller usually works on commission and is eager to have as many successful quote responses possible.

Buyers can post requests for quotation on the site by filling in the blanks on an on-line form. Buyers can then save the form and publish it for all the registered sellers to observe. After a quote request is published, the sellers are able to read the details of the request on the site and initiate a response by the click of a mouse.

For sellers this site provides a response form that guides the seller toward giving a best-quote response with an accurate price and confirmation of terms. For both buyers and sellers this site maintains historical databases for a one-year period so they can review the quote requests they created and the quote responses they made.

In addition, the site includes an ongoing discussion database for providing questions and answers on each quote request. If sellers have any questions on a quote request they can post their questions on the site and the buyers can respond. If buyers wish to provide additional information to the sellers, they can use the same discussion database to post a comment. There is special feature in the quote request area that enables buyers to extend the deadline date for or publish an addendum to a quote request.

Purchasing Online provides a public discussion database for all buyers and sellers where purchasing issues in general can be discussed. The issues can be organized by area of business, product category, or where they fit into the chronological purchasing process (i.e., researching, preparing, or responding to RFPs, negotiating, making awards, shipping, disposing of surplus, etc.) The discussion database has a threaded format that connects topics with their subsequent comments for ease of response. The database also has keyword search capability for finding items of interest.

Purchasing Online provides an area where sellers can advertise specials. Buyers can sort the special items in various ways. They can list the items by product category or seller company name, or search for items with a keyword.

Purchasing Online provides a question-and-answer forum for posing and answering questions from members of the Purchasing Online community, and forums for posting jobs, events, or activities that may be of interest to buyers and sellers.[21]

Company: Oracle Corp.
Product: Fast Forward Internet Procurement (FFIP)
Procurement application: Oracle's Web page describes FFIP as a fully automated Web-based procurement solution for small and mid-size companies. It's designed to reduce purchasing costs by 10 percent and cut processing by 50 percent, says Oracle. FFIP, which takes 60 days to get up and running, includes software modules, on-site training, a year of full-time support, and extranet links to the

suppliers: Corporate Express for office products and Grainger for industrial products.[22]

Company: PartNET
Product: eCommerce
Procurement application: According to PartNET's Web page, PartNET technology gives you the power to bring together commercial information from multiple suppliers into a catalog tailored to your organization's buying needs. A PartNET catalog is unique because it aggregates in multiple real-time distributed data sources. With PartNET eCommerce, catalog information from any number of suppliers, anywhere on the Internet, can be unified into a single virtual catalog. The products and pricing listed in your catalog are specific to your company; the reach and breadth of the Web leverages your buying power. Because of the power of PartNET's technology, the United States Department of Defense chose PartNET to build its EMall.[23]

Company: Procureit
Product: ProcureIT
Procurement application: According to ProcureIT's Web page, this product is an enterprise-wide electronic-procurement and MRO solution that automates the entire purchasing and materials-management process. This Web-based Intranet application is deployed directly to individual user desktops.

The following modules are available with ProcureIT:

> On-line Requisitioning, Purchase and Audit Module
> Task-Scheduling Module
> Inventory Module
> Asset-Tracking Module
> Kitting & Assembly Module
> Internal-Messaging Module
> Standing-Order Module

Rule-Builder Module
Standard-Reports Module
Crystal-Reports Module
QuikLoad Mass-Data-Loading Module
RFQ Module
Fax Module
EDI Module

Because it is 100% browser-based, every aspect of ProcureIT is point-and-click. Even novices can log on and be productive in minutes, which means that it doesn't take a rocket scientist to order rocket parts.[24]

Company: ProcureNet
Product: OneSource Procurement
Procurement application: ProcureNet's Web page indicates that the OneSource Procurement desktop-purchasing and materials-management system manages all steps of the purchasing process: requisition processing, inventory management, bid processing, purchase orders, asset management, invoicing, and accounts-payable processing.

OneSource SmartCatalog offers a parametrically searchable catalog that contains frequently purchased MRO items from approved vendors. For products not in this client-specific catalog, end users can access OneSource PurchasePlace, ProcureNet's own catalog of MRO items with negotiated prices from ProcureNet's vendors.

If an item is not in either catalog, OneSource Integrated Spot Buy gives end users access to ProcureNet's team of professional buyers, who will find the item and negotiate with the vendor for the best possible price. Once an item is sourced, it is added to ProcureNet's PurchasePlace catalog, a process that will reduce non-catalog buys over time.[25]

Company: PurchasePro.com
Product: PurchasePro.com
Procurement application: PurchasePro's Web page describes PurchasePro as a standard platform for small and medium-sized businesses, as well as corporate purchasing departments, to buy and sell products in secure, on-line, open or private marketplaces. It is an electronic marketplace of thousands of companies that communicate with each other via e-commerce. These companies shop and create catalogs, send and receive bids, and place and fulfill orders -- using a standard Internet connection.[26]

Company: PurchasingCenter.com
Product: a low-cost Web portal, or "work center," for MRO buyers
Procurement application: This low-cost, Web-based service that delivers the necessary information, commerce, and productivity tools to support the complete requirements of effective MRO management. It supports the information, procurement, and process requirements of MRO buyers and plant and facilities maintenance workers. PurchasingCenter.com's portal is built on four pillars. These include: 1) Content about MRO buying news, career information, job listings, and supplier and product directories. The portal also provides OSHA requirements, equipment and product specs, supplier ratings, and application notes. 2)Community: which establishes a virtual channel for maintenance professionals to exchange information on products, equipment specifications, and buying strategies. 3) Tools: a utility that enables a user to create and manage a private "Purchasing Page" for sharing information with suppliers. and 4) Commerce: PurchasingCenter.com supports repeat orders, sourcing, and spot buys, which account for a large portion of MRO spending. Users can place orders through the portal's catalog of over 100,000 MRO items or use a sourcing tool to locate suppliers by manufacturer, brand, category, or location. Users can also design and distribute RFQs to preferred and new suppliers, and to manage negotiations. The portal also supports auctions for the sale of excess inventories.

Company: Remedy Corp.

Product: Remedy Purchasing@Work

Procurement application: Remedy's Web page indicates that the product creates on-line catalogs that bring multiple suppliers together on-screen for product selection and pricing availability, and it provides for placing orders on line. The product automatically creates audit trails to track supplier performance and employee buying patterns. It lets users enter, route, and track purchase requisitions and orders on line.

The software is configurable so that automatic routing and approvals conform to a company's purchasing policies. Once a purchase requisition is submitted, Remedy Purchasing@Work automatically routes requests according to a company's existing approval rules. An intuitive Web browser interface provides easy access through the Employee Workplace Intranet portal, which gives employees a central location for submitting purchase requisitions. The portal provides management with access to all reports and purchase requests pending approval. Users can check inventory levels, order statuses, and delivery information.

Remedy estimates that a customer with 5,000 purchase requests per year will see a positive return on investment within six months.[27]

Company: SAP, Inc.

Product: SAP R/3; mySAP.com

Procurement application: According to SAP's Web page, SAP-R/3 covers all processes, from the creation of a requisition, with or without catalogs, to the payment of the invoice. All end users are able to purchase goods and services straight from their desktops.

mySAP.com, a business directory, provides network information on buyers and sellers, as well as company information, product catalogs, contacts, and target-market data. The business directory enables any company to register itself at the mySAP.com marketplace. In addition to supplying address and contact information, a company can categorize itself using UNPC product and service categories and subcategorizes. This feature will make it easy for potential suppliers and customers to find a company and its products and services.

The document exchange feature provides a seamless, one-step way for buyers and sellers to exchange information in the marketplace. It will provide additional data fields that a company can maintain, which will enable seamless execution of a business process. In a buyer-seller scenario, the selling party can add vendor or supplier master data to its entry in the business directory. On the buying side, this information will be used to create a vendor master record for the supplier in the buyer's ERP system, in the background. This process takes place during the purchase-requisition process. It enables integration of the purchase request into the accounts-payable process of the buying company.

mySAP.com's RFP and RFQ matching provides a central location to post, distribute, and match RFPs and RFQs. mySAP.com enables you to research and match the needs of your buyers with the capabilities of your suppliers through an intelligent classification system. Using mySAP.com, companies can also distribute RFP and RFQ changes without having to photocopy and mail a new copy of the document each time it changes.

mySAP.com will aggregate both buyers and sellers into two on-line auction types: cross-industry markets and industry-specific markets. In both areas, mySAP.com will offer open and private markets. Customers can benefit from auctions that help clear excess inventory.[28]

Company: SAS Institute
Product: SAS Solution for Supplier Relationship Management (SRM)
Procurement application: According to SAS's Web page, SRM merges all procurement information for both direct and indirect purchases from disparate systems across the enterprise. Using comprehensive and advanced data-warehousing tools, the system has access to all transactional information from such sources as legacy systems,

ERP applications, and E-commerce implementations, and brings it together into a single procurement information warehouse.

SRM allows buyers to standardize all supplier and commodity information so that their procurement-information warehouses contain one global view of their data. SRM combines with Dun and Bradstreet's D&B D-U-N-S© Number and the United Nations Standard Product and Service Classification (UN/SPSC) to allow for one universal language; that way any organization can understand the procurement information intellectually.

Dun and Bradstreet also uses a universal purchasing code, Standard Product and Services Codes (SPSC TM). The SPSC allows customers effectively to identify potential and existing suppliers and the products and services they provide.[29]

Company: SciQuest.com
Product: Custom Purchasing Solutions
Procurement application: According to SciQuest's Web page, their database has hundreds of suppliers with over 200,000 available products. Custom on-line catalogs display the products and suppliers you choose and the prices negotiated with them. Buyers can search catalogs, place orders, and track shipments on line.

The system allows you to set spending limits and follow purchase-approval routing according to your organization's needs. It integrates with current purchasing and finance systems.

Each order placed to SciQuest.com can include as many different suppliers and products as needed. The system consolidates the paperwork. Frequently ordered supplies can be stored in a special link called Your Favorites.

Various detailed reports can be generated to best analyze your organization's spending activities, which will help you to manage your purchasing power more effectively. Reports can be created by the categories you want, such as department code, commodity code, individual lab, or user, as well as many others. Install and use the system at no cost. There are no setup charges and no user fees.[30]

Company: Solix

Product: iOperations

Procurement application: According to Solix's Web page, iOPerations is a full, on-line procurement software package that combines a procurement engine with modules for travel planning, expense reporting, payment collection, and other self-service applications for human resources.

The Operations package works with back-end ERP business systems from Baan, Oracle, PeopleSoft, and SAP.[31]

Company: Supplybase

Product: Supplybase.manager

Procurement application: Supplybase.inc's Web page indicates that the target group for this product is a company's engineers, procurement professionals, and suppliers. Supplybase .manager provides engineers and procurement professionals with the ability to share project, part, supplier, and process information easily. Event-driven triggers monitor the development of the particular parts of a user's projects and provide quick and easy access to supplier information for each part. Reporting on users, parts, projects, supplier efficiency, and tooling management can be generated and shared across the organization. Tools used for custom part development at supplier sites can be tracked by engineers. They can also obtain updates from suppliers on the capacity and condition of the tool, notifications on tool capacity shortages, tooling end of life, and tooling cost forecasts. Supplybase.manager creates and manages a repository of information enabling manufacturers to monitor and track the costs, time, and activities specific to the business interactions with their approved suppliers.

Supplybase.manager generates and maintains dynamic supplier scorecards, which document supplier efficiency and performance.

Suppliers can update their own information including contact, facility, and technology-related information, thus keeping their customers aware of dynamic changes to both process and manufacturing capabilities at the supplier site. Customer feedback incorporated into supplier scorecards provides suppliers with performance information in order to facilitate continuous improvement.

Quick identification and qualification of suppliers worldwide via the Web 24/7 gives engineers instant and reliable knowledge for faster and better decision making. Supplybase.central's 35 strategic commodities commodities include plastics, metals, cabling, power supplies, and other engineering-intensive commodities that significantly affect development times. Global coverage of over 250,000 suppliers of custom parts includes South East Asia, China, Central/Eastern Europe, and North America. Supplybase.central is augmented with insightful information on suppliers, including financial and risk analysis from leading providers of market-focused business information, such as Dun & Bradstreet and Cahners Publications.[32]

Company: SupplierMarket
Product: SupplierMarket.com
Procurement Application: SupplierMarket.com is an online marketplace for built-to-order industrial products that include looking to source a new part or finding a new business. Buyers can write standardized request for quotes (RFQ) online, review pre-qualified suppliers' capabilities and choose suppliers after online bidding sessions.

Suppliers are automatically matched with RFQs, can submit online bids in a live bidding session and win business with minimal prospecting costs.

According to SupplerMarket.com, buyer benefits include a reduction in costs of procurement by 15-20%, unlimited access to a group of new, qualified suppliers, competitive advantages by shortening procurement processes and a decreased amount of time you spend finding suppliers.

Supplier benefits include reduced sales cycles and virtual elimination of prospecting costs, access to a large number of qualified RFQs, ability to compete for a buyer's business on a level playing filed, ability to quickly fill excess capacity and do all of this without any investment in new technology.[33]

Company: Technical Services Associates Inc. (TSA)
Product: Gateway Client Server
Procurement application: This is a Windows-based client/server purchasing software application designed to meet requirements for medium- to large-sized operations. It includes on-line requisitioning, purchase orders, vendor data, receiving, and reporting processes. TSA also has modules available for asset management, inventory, and accounts payable.

Gateway Client Server allows you to create, edit, and track documents throughout each step of the purchasing process, while additional modules allow you to tailor the system to more precisely meet your needs.

The system design is geared toward providing a simple, straightforward process for the end user to enter purchase requests, forward those requests for approval, and then forward them to purchasing. Key elements of the requisition entry include a header screen that captures general information about the requisition and a detail screen that provides for defining the items to be purchased.

Standard routing and approvals are provided for requisitions based on the department to which the requisitioner belongs, and the amount that an individual may authorize. The amounts and departments are controlled by system tables. The user profile establishes an amount that a requisitioner or approver can authorize, and also establishes the department with which the requisitioner is associated.

Orders can be created from scratch, a previously entered requisition, or the results of an RFQ. When creating an order from a requisition or an RFQ, the system displays a list of candidates from which to select.

The system provides a comprehensive supplier management capability that is based on one supplier ID with multiple addresses and multiple contacts. Purchase history display and supplier performance are fully integrated.

The system provides a catalog function for selecting line items on requisitions, RFQs, and purchase orders. Catalogs provide a quick and simple means for choosing the required items. Catalogs can be developed in-house or provided by suppliers in a TSA-specified format. Any number of catalogs can be loaded. Some examples of commonly used catalogs are Furniture, Workstation, Office Supplies, and Computer Supplies. Catalogs can also be tied to blanket orders so that any requisition placed against the catalog will automatically produce and send a release order to the supplier without purchasing's intervention.[34]

Company: Trilogy Software
Product: Buying Chain
Procurement application: According to Trilogy's Web page, Buying Chain is used for midsize businesses, it includes suppliers such as Barnesandnoble.com, CompUSA, and Office Depot. Buying Chain's supplier network boasts over 150 leading suppliers with over twenty million products, including computers, office equipment, travel services, books, and industrial supplies.

Buying Chain generates comprehensive data and reports on supplier performance. It has analysis tools that allow organizations to track and measure company spending by user, department, cost center, or any other company-specific method.

Buying Chain can be downloaded, installed, and deployed for any company's needs in a few hours. Through the use of wizards and graphical interfaces, Buying Chain maintenance requires no programming, allowing non-technical administrators easily to configure and assign rules, customize catalogs, and manage user data.[35]

Company: Works.com.Inc.
Product: Works.com
Procurement Application: According to its Web page, Works.com is an on-line procurement offering that essentially asks buyers to

change suppliers in exchange for efficiency and savings. Works.com will offer office products from S.P. Richards Co. (a unit of Genuine Parts Co.), one of the largest U.S. office products wholesalers, which sells mainly to businesses such as Boise Cascade Office Products, Corporate Express, and Office Depot. The Works.com catalog of 20,000 products includes furniture, janitorial products, and office supplies.

Works.com is for companies with 250 to 500 employees, whether small to medium-sized businesses or branches of larger companies. Works.com charges the buyer $1.50 per order for its service.[36]

References

[1]Agentics Web page.

[2]American Software Web page.

[3]Purchasing on-line, June 1999.

[4]Aspect Web page.

[5]Ton Stein, Information Week;April 26, 1999, Issue: 731; Section: Software Enterprise On The Web -- Baan Suite To Help Extend Software.

[6]Brio Web page.

[7]Buyers zone Web page.

[8]Chemdex Web page.

[9]Internet Week Online; Thursday, August 19, 1999, Clarus Changes E-Procurement Rules, Richard Karpinski And Claus Web page.

[10]ConnectInc. Web page.

[11]Dazel WebPage.

[12]Clinton Wilder, Information Week April 26, 1999, Issue: 731, Section: Intranets/Internet Easier Web Procurement -- Digital Buyer, Targets Production Supplies.

[13]Elcom Web page.

[14]FairMarket Web page.

[15]Free Market Web page.

[16]GE Web page.

[17]WebFOCUS Web page.

[18]Intelisys Web page.

[19]Clinton Wilder, Information Week, Technology News: Intelisys, Oracle To Improve Procurement Products.

[20]Netscape Web page.

[21]NetReq Web page.

[22]Oracle Web page.

[23]Electronic Buyers News, April 19, 1999, Issue: 1156, Section: Supply-Chain Management.

[24]Procureit Web page.

[25]ProcureNet Web page.
[26]PurchsePro Web page.
[27]Remedy Web page.
[28]SAP Web page.
[29]SAS Institute Web page.
[30]SciQuest web page.
[31]Richard Karpinski, Technology News: Solix Goes Beyond Online Procurement By Tom Stein, Information Week Internet Week, May 17, 1999, Issue: 765, Section: News & Analysis; E-Commerce Tools, Standards Alleviate.
[32]Supplybase.inc Web page.
[33]SupplierMarket Web page.
[34]Technical Services Associates Web page.
[35]Trilogy Web page.
[36]Works.com Web page.
Tom Stein, Information Week Internet Week: May 17, 1999, Issue: 765; Section: News & Analysis; E-Commerce Tools, Standards Alleviate Richard Karpinski

Section 4
The Future of
e-Puchasing

14

The Future of e-Purchasing

The novelist William Gibson was right when he said that there's no need to predict the future. The future is already here.

Surf's Up! Catch the Wave

As you have read over and over again in this text, information technologies are having a drastic impact on the way businesses buy and sell goods and services. Purchasers and suppliers realize that they must adopt such technologies in order to survive and grow in an increasingly competitive environment. The world of purchasing will be forever changed due to the impact of these various technologies. It's not enough to surf the World Wide Web; it's time to ride it to e-Purchasing success!

While the popular press spends a lot of time discussing the consumer's movement to on-line shopping, that wave is dwarfed by the impact of ever-increasing business-to-business transactions. For example, research shows that consumers spent over 3 billion on the Internet in 1998.[1] The combined on-line business volume of General Electric, Dell, and Cisco, however, totalled 3 billion

Dollars.[2] The U. S. Department of Commerce expects total business-to-business e-commerce to exceed 300 billion dollars in three to five years.

IBM chairman Louis Gerstner claims there will be 200 million people on the 'net at the end of 1999, and 500 million connected users by 2003. These numbers will change the way most firms approach their customers and, more importantly for the readers of this text, the way they approach their suppliers in configuring an electronic supply chain. The Internet is changing not only corporate America but corporations worldwide.

This truly global marketplace, combined with company intranets and extranets, is providing purchasing with powerful tools to change drastically the way companies do business. These tools will bring about untold productivity benefits and eliminate mundane clerical and transactional tasks that have often kept purchasing out of the strategic environment. The Internet may be the ultimate driver that enables purchasing to become a major value-adding strategic contributor to the firm. Historically purchasing was viewed by upper management as a clerical or administrative function. The bottom line is that purchasers must now add strategic value to their work or their jobs will be outsourced to a technology-savvy, independent buying firm that already has it.

Technology helps buyers become more productive and cpompanies save money by allowing cross-organizational transactions to take place much more efficiently. This in turn creates a truly extended-enterprise environment by giving suppliers and customers access to information that was previously considered solely internal. One major corporation, for example, allows its suppliers to enter its intranet and access engineering information on specifications and schedules. The company continually performs system updates in order to keep lead times and prices current.

Now that you have an understanding of the technology you can understand the emergence of extranets and intranets. Extranets (external internets) are being used by many firms in new ways to coordinate the activities of suppliers, purchasers, and customers.

Extranets allow firms to provide their best customers with access to pricing, latest designs, inventory information, and lead times. Suppliers are also allowed access to the supply-side portion of the extranets to update their lead times, check any design changes, get scheduling information, and provide replenishments of orders. Meanwhile, intranets (internal networks) provide information that all members inside the organization can access regarding training, company policies, standard forms, and personnel issues.

What the Experts Are Predicting

The views of two experts, who are very close to these trends, provide important insights. First we'll look at IBM Chairman Lou Gerstner's views regarding the creation of a new e-business economy that is partially driven by the convergence of computing and communications. Second, Don Tapscott, best-selling author of six books, including *The Digital Economy and Growing Up Digital*, and chairman of the Alliance for Converging Technologies, a research think tank funded by many of the world's leading technology, manufacturing, retail, financial, and government organizations.

The following is a extract of a keynote speech given by the Chairman of IBM, Lou Gerstner at Telecom 99. Gerstner discusses the creation of a new economy, the eBusiness Economy. A major step to the new economy is the convergence of computing and communications.

According to Gerstner, conservative estimates say Internet commerce will easily exceed $1 trillion in the next few years, representing somewhere between 5 and 10 percent of all business transactions worldwide. And this is not just a US phenomenon. Europe's share of global Web commerce, for example, was 11 percent last year, headed to 33 percent by 2003.

The eBusiness economy isn't built solely on online retail sales of books or airline tickets or securities. Some of the most important Net-based transactions are not very visible. These include transactions among employees within businesses, across supply chains, or online procurement applications, as well as the vital online transactions in the public sector -- in health care, education and government services.

There's already a tremendous amount of e-marketplace activity in vertical industries -- in metals, petrochemical, plastics, semi-conductors, tools. In the market for chemicals used by life sciences companies, the best paper catalog contains 60,000 products from hundreds of suppliers and is updated yearly. Now there's a global market -- a digital market -- with more than five times as many products and everything including prices is updated daily.

Gerstner added " we're just four or five years into the development of a new economy that will mature over a quarter century or more. So whether these e-marketplaces and exchanges will prove to be experiments, interim steps, or meteors that flame out before our eyes, who knows?[3]

Purchasing in the Future:

The e-business economy will bring a variety of inherent conflicts and changes to purchasing organizations:

1. The move toward reduction of the supplier base vs. the ability for thousands of suppliers worldwide to quote on requirements.
2. Developing long-term relationships with suppliers vs. significant cost reductions by selecting the lowest-cost supplier from the world market.
3. Paper contracts vs. on-line virtual contracts.
4. Continual reduction of price from technological advances.

These contradictions will most likely be addressed by segmenting and applying specific commodities to each conflict. For example, non-production and MRO buying will lean toward needing suppliers worldwide to quote on equipment, while production-type commodities will continue to need the basic supply relationships with a reduced number of suppliers for strategic suppliers. The other production suppliers will also benefit from the availability of multiple suppliers world wide.

The Rise of the 'Net Generation'

Lou Gerstner sees e-business from the viewpoint of chief executive for a leading technology firm. Don Tapscott provides futuristic insight from the perspective of a leader paid to research these trends. In his book *Growing up Digital* Tapscott introduces the "'net generation": eighty-eight million offspring produced by the 85 million baby boomers. What makes this generation different from its predecessors is that it is the first to grow up surrounded by digital media. Computers and other digital technologies, such as digital cameras, are commonplace to "n-gen" members. They work with them at home and in school, and they use them for entertainment. Increasingly these technologies are connected to the Internet, an expanding web of networks that is attracting a million new users monthly. Constantly surrounded by technology, today's kids are accustomed to its strong presence in their lives. And it is through their use of the digital media that the n-gen will develop and superimpose its culture on the rest of society.[4]

Following are several themes from Tapscott's books and their impact on purchasing in the future.

Information about Information

Tapscott's theme -- Voice communication with the computer will become a way of life. Active software agents will search the 'net based on criteria we establish and will generate information about information.[5]

Purchasing in the future -- When a buyer turns on his computer he will be welcomed with, "Good morning, John. Let me update you on what's happened overnight in the semiconductor industry. Your vendor Hatachi just announced a product that you can use. Your Purchase Order number 12345 was just shipped by UPS and will be at the local UPS terminal by noon today. I found a great buy for the assembly you were looking for yesterday: Assembly Co. of New Zealand can provide these parts at 15 percent less than our current supplier."

Characteristics of the Future Purchasing Professional

Tapscott's theme -- The 'net generation is exceptionally curious, self-reliant, contrarian, smart, focused, able to adapt, high in self-esteem, and has a global orientation. They also have worries about the future. They mistrust the government and the elite. They value individual freedoms and rights highly, including the right to be left alone, the right to privacy, the right to have and express their own views. They are globally oriented and open minded. They have a great desire to be connected with their families and close friends, in school, neighborhoods, interest groups, and on-line virtual communities. They love their music, movies, magazines, some TV shows, video games, computers, software, and the 'net. These attributes, combined with the n-geners' ease with digital tools, spell trouble for the traditional enterprise and the traditional manager. This generation will create huge pressure for radical change in existing companies.[5]

Purchasing in the future -- The future professional purchaser will: be very independent; prefer to work alone and be an individual contributor rather than part of a team; prefer to work much of the time at home; have such high esteem that he will be willing to reveal his innermost thoughts; have already been an expert on a topic of importance as a child and thus will favor peer-oriented relationships rather than hierarchies; be an authority in one area and a student in another; and be attracted to companies that are perceived as ethical and acting in the community interest.[6]

Organizational Structure / Compensation

Tapscott's theme -- The 'net generation will expect to be compensated based on contribution rather than position in the hierarchy.[7]

Purchasing in the future -- The organization will be flat, with many professionals reporting to one "manager." Compensation will no longer be based on the number of people reporting to a manager, but rather on one's contribution. Thus many professionals will have higher compensation than their managers.

Different Processes for Different Countries

Tapscott's theme -- There is a growing gap between have and have-not nations. Most 'net users are in the United States. Europe (except Scandinavia) and Japan are far behind. Tiger economies in Asia are leapfrogging Europe and Japan. But the real gap lies between the developed and developing worlds.[8]

Purchasing in the future -- There will be different sets of buying rules for different nations. Systems will require the capabilities of connecting with worldwide suppliers via the Web or via fax, and with others via telephone only. The sophistication of supplier systems could influence which specific suppliers a company purchases from, especially if a company decides that all suppliers must be able to communicate via the Web.

Office Environment

Tapscott's theme -- 'Net generation workers will be able to work at their customers' locations, from their car, in a restaurant, or from their vacation homes.[9]

Purchasing in the future -- Buyers will be at suppliers' locations, suppliers will be at buyers' locations, and there will be less of a need for a company to have large amounts of office space, since much of the work may take place in home offices.

Real-Time, On-line-Customer Environment

Tapscott's theme -- There will be a need for continuous and immediate adjustment to customer demands, supplier capabilities, and business conditions. Customer orders will arrive electronically, then be automatically processed. Chips will be imbedded in everything, producing real-time, immediate feedback. For example, a dress shirt's embedded chip will talk to the washing machine and tell it to add more soap as the shirt evaluates it own cleanliness.[10]

Purchasing in the future -- Automated customer orders will generate automatic supplier Purchase Orders. Just In Time will be universal and will require little need for warehousing. Buyers will perform multiple tasks in "real time," involving different people, multiple information sources, and a variety of applications running concurrently. Buyer/supplier chat rooms will be common and will include suppliers communicating directly with their own and the customers' manufacturing operations. When the last item is used on a line, a process will be triggered to release more parts automatically.

How Do I Ride This Wave?

The goal of this text was to provide you with an understanding of e-Purchasing and some steps on how to get the process started. There is a lack of literature available about how successfully to introduce and implement e-Purchasing. There is, however, a great deal of information on the benefits and opportunities available in e-purchasing, which you might use to sell management on the need to test these waters and move forward toward your new business model. We understand that mere access to these technologies will not in itself be enough for you to transform your organization; access must be coupled with significant process changes. We hope this book helps the reader to understand not only e-Purchasing technologies, but also how a company's processes need to be changed in order to take advantage of the mega changes that are occurring in the new electronic business environment.

References

[1]Internet is Opening up a New Era of Pricing, Wall Street Journal, p 1, February 13, 1999.

[2]Internet is Opening up a New Era of Pricing, Wall Street Journal, p 1, February 13, 1999.

[3]Taken from Lou Gerstner?s keynote remarks at Telecom 99

[4]Don Tapscott, *Growing up Digital*, McGraw Hill, New York, 1998

[5]Don Tapscott, pp. 32 -33

[6]Don Tapscott, p.

[7]Don Tapscott, p. 212

[8]Don Tapscott, pp. 224-259

[9]Don Tapscott, p. 16

[10]Don Tapscott, p. 222

Appendix A
-- Useful URLs

Listed below are URLs appropriate for the purchasing function. Several URLs were provided by Bendorf & Associates Purchasing Consultants, who specialize in consulting and training in management, purchasing, supply chain, global sourcing, international procurement, and developing world-class purchasing operations. Visit Bendorf & Associates' Web page (www.bendorf.com) for hot links to many of the URLs below.

www.advmfg.com

Advanced Manufacturing Research -- Helping clients make informed decisions critical to managing the total manufacturing enterprise.

www.apics.com

The official Web site of APICS (American Production and Inventory Control Society), the educational society for resource management.

www.arnet.gov/far

Federal Acquisitions Regulations (FAR). You can review this site for the complete Federal Acquisition Regulations. More stuff than you ever wanted but some good procedures and definitions are

223

contained in FAR that could save you time if you are developing a manual. If your firm is selling to the government, this information can be helpful in understanding their requirements. Source: Bendorf and Associates (www.bendorf.com).

www.asiansources.com

Asian Sources -- Infomediary between purchases around the world and suppliers in Asia.

www.btopi.com

A full-service distributor of office products serving mainly medium- and large-size businesses, institutions, and government agencies. SyntraNet is their on-line catalog, which can be browsed by item, category, or manufacturer. Must have an account to order on line. With an account you can create order templates for frequently ordered items and view listings of recently ordered items. Source: Bendorf and Associates (www.bendorf.com).

www.brokerforum.com

The Broker Forum, Inc., provides sourcing tools for independent distributors. The site collects entire inventory databases and allows members to search for parts and contact the seller to negotiate the purchase.

www.capsresearch.org

Center for Advanced Purchasing Studies (CAPS) is a nonprofit organization that, while affiliated with the National Association of Purchasing Management and the Arizona State University College of Business, is an independent research organization. Its mission is to help organizations achieve competitive advantage by providing them with leading-edge research to support the evolution of strategic purchasing and supply management.

www.catalog.com/napmsv

NAPM Silicon Valley -- Provides an extensive list of URLs

by purchasing category.

www.census.gov/pub/epcd/www/naicsusr.html
      The North American Industry Classification System will provide common industry definitions for Canada, Mexico, and the U.S. The new system will replace what has commonly been known as industry SIC codes. This site provides a variety of information about the upcoming changes and related business issues. Source: Bendorf and Associates (www.bendorf.com).

www.chemconnect.com
      Connects chemical buyers and sellers.

www.chemequipmag.com
      Products, systems, and services for the chemical industry.

www.chipcenter.com
      ChipCenter -- Arrow, Avnet, and Marshall teamed up to provide parts for electronic engineers and purchasers.

www.CHIPSOURCE.com
      Maintains parts databases exclusively for independent distributors and brokers.

www.virtualpet.com
      A compilation of tools and resources available on the Web to assist you in research. Tools include a 13-step process of research basics that gives you tips about the best way to do research on line. Includes links to relevant Web sites in the search process and also references printed sources when not available on the Web. Examples of sites listed: Census Bureau, Federal Data SIC Codes, SEC Filings, Thomas Register, and many more sites for seeking

information on a particular company. Source: Bendorf and Associates (www.bendorf.com).

www.developages.com

Enables sourcing and purchasing professionals to find and evaluate suppliers of custom parts and assemblies.

www.digitalmarket.com

Digital Market, Inc.-- Enterprise software solution for large companies that want to create their own supply-chain extranets so that potential suppliers can come to them.

www.dow.com

Financial Information on companies.

www.fairmarket.com

FairMarket Inc.-- Sets up auctions on line.

www.fastexchange.com

Automates the purchase of simple off-the-shelf electronic components from 4000 vendors.

www.fastparts.com

FastParts.Com -- Brings together sellers of surplus component inventory with buyers relying on electronic bulletin boards.

www.FASTPARTS.com

Fast Parts, Chicago -- Trading exchange for electronic parts and components.

www.freemarkets.com

Free Markets of Pittsburgh is one of the leading providers of on-line auctions and bidding for organizational buyers in the public and private sectors.

www.ftechg.com or ftginfo@ftgchg.com

Provides information about Fisher Technologies suite of e-purchasing applications and solutions, such as Cornerstone.

www.knowx.com

Public records on the Web (purchasing laws, suits, and UCC findings).

www.industry.net

Industry net -- A resourceful information center for businesses and industry professionals. Membership is free and allows you access to 3,000 business centers links, searchable catalogs of 20,000 manufacturers and distributors, interactive forums, and trade association information.

Source: Bendorf and Associates (www.bendorf.com).

www.iso.com

This site is a resource for standards such as ISO 9000, ANSI, and DIN. Electrical and electronic standards are not covered.

Source: Bendorf and Associates (www.bendorf.com).

www.metalworld.com

RecycleNet Metal -- Offers buyers access to 42 categories of metals.

www.napm.org

The National Association of Purchasing Management home page. Tons of great stuff for members, including articles, jobs, speakers, consultants, seminars, etc.

www.ncmahq.org

National Contract Management Association -- Information about membership, job referrals, certification, and related links.

Source: Bendorf and Associates (www.bendorf.com).

www.netbuyparts.com

Spot market for electronic components.

www.netcomponents.com

Database of over 300 electronics distributors. Must be a registered member to use the site. Gives you access to a distributor's inventory and allows you to see what quantity of a specific part the distributor will have on hand as of a specified date. Source: Bendorf and Associates (www.bendorf.com).

www.netmind.com

Manages information -- Allows for automatic receipt of changes when tracked pages change.

www.newspage.com

Market intelligence

www.nigp.org

National Institute of Government Purchasing -- A nonprofit educational organization dedicated to helping governments buy. Source: Bendorf and Associates (www.bendorf.com).

www.nyu.edu/purchasing.services

New York University -- The Web site for the NYU purchasing department, with links to the purchasing departments of other universities. Source: Bendorf and Associates (www.bendorf.com).

Npi.purchasing.co.harris.tx.us

National Purchasing Institute -- Newsletter for government, educational, and institutional Professionals. Source: Bendorf and Associates (www.bendorf.com).

www.obi.com

Open Buying on the Internet (OBI) -- A consortium has established a common architecture to guide companies and vendors in implementing Internet-based purchasing systems. Open Buying on the Internet, 400005 Mirand Ave. Suite 175, Palo Alto, CA 94304.

www.outsourcing.com

Association founded in 1993 for objective, independent

information on the strategic use of outside resources. For the site to provide useful information, you need to become registered as a member of the institute. Source: Bendorf and Associates (www.bendorf.com).

www.procurenet.com

A user-friendly MRO business-to-business mall that claims to be the one-stop buying solution to all your MRO buying needs. Site has over 125 suppliers offering 300,000 products in five areas: lab equipment and supplies, electrical equipment and supplies, industrial equipment, clinical supplies, and professional services.

www.purchasing.com

The magazine for total supply-chain management.

www.purchasing.about.com

Information about the purchasing profession.

www.purchasingcenter.com

Business-to-business Web site focusing on the needs of industrial-supply buyers in mid-sized companies and departments of larger organizations. Provides articles, supplier directory, excess inventory auctions, and quotations.

www.purchasingguide.com

Purchasing Guide -- The Purchasing Guide offers access to its database of over 130,000 suppliers. Helps corporate and government purchasing professionals find suppliers by product, service description, or a number of other criteria, including SIC code or federal supply code. The user can also further narrow his search by business size, minority/woman-owned business, and state or federally qualified. Registration is free. Source: Bendorf and Associates (www.bendorf.com).

www.purchasingonline.com

Connects business and government professionals who buy and sell goods for their respective companies or organizations. It provides neutral and impartial services to professional buyers and sellers, including:

• Discussion Topics Forum for professional buyers and sellers to discuss issues regarding the purchasing and selling process. Registered buyers and sellers can create new topics or respond to existing topics in this forum, which is searchable and categorized by specific topics for ease of research.

• Request for Quotation Service (the primary activity on the site) provides the on-line capability for buyers to advertise requests for quotation and for sellers to respond to those requests. It eliminates the manual processes of mailing, faxing, and telephone calls formerly needed in order to complete a request for quotation.

www.powersourcing.com

Tool available for finding and contacting suppliers. Suppliers have hot links to their Web pages.

www.recycle.net

Recycle World -- This site is basically an on-line list of want ads advertising either available or wanted scrap metals. You can post an ad in four categories of metal: Iron and Steel, Non-Ferrous Metals, Precious Metals, and Exotic Metals. Listings are free and left on the site for 30 days. You can also buy, trade, and sell other recycled materials at the site, such as wood, batteries, and computers. Source: Bendorf and Associates (www.bendorf.com).

www.reportgallery.com

Search engine for annual reports.

www.RFQdata.com

An inexpensive and easy-to-use tool for buyers and sellers.

Superpages.gte.net

GTE super pages -- Contains a number of great features for locating businesses across the U.S. The database has 5,000 Yellow Pages directories for locating any business' Web site. Can create full-color drawing maps and directions (up to 200 miles) from any address or zip code. Has access to a Lycos city guide for local information on the 450 largest cities in the U.S. Has begun a classified ads page that currently lists vehicles, computers, real estate, and more for sale. Source: Bendorf and Associates (www.bendorf.com). www.thomasregister.com

Thomas Register on line.

www.traveler.net

Reed Publishing's TravelerNet -- Overview of travel and related Web sites.

Index